the pop classics series

let's go exploring.
calvin
and
hobbes
michael hingston

ecwpress

Published by ECW Press
665 Gerrard Street East
Toronto, Ontario, Canada M4M 1Y2
416-694-3348 / info@ecwpress.com

Editors for the press:
Jennifer Knoch and Crissy Calhoun
Cover and text design: David Gee
Series proofreader: Avril McMeekin

Library and Archives Canada
Cataloguing in Publication

Hingston, Michael, 1985–, author
Let's go exploring : Calvin and Hobbes /
Michael Hingston.

(Pop classics ; 10)
Includes bibliographical references.
Issued in print and electronic formats.
ISBN 978-1-77041-413-6 (softcover).
Also issued as: 978-1-77305-180-2 (PDF),
ISBN 978-1-77305-179-6 (ePUB)

1. Watterson, Bill. Calvin and Hobbes.
2. Comic books, strips, etc. — United States.
I. Title. II. Series: Pop classics series ; 10

PN6728.C34H56 2018   741.5'6973
C2017-906585-8   C2017-906586-6

Printing: Friesens   5 4 3 2 1
PRINTED AND BOUND IN CANADA

The publication of *Let's Go Exploring* has been generously supported by the Government of
Canada through the Canada Book Fund. *Ce livre est financé en partie par le gouvernement
du Canada.* We also acknowledge the contribution of the Government of Ontario through the
Ontario Book Publishing Tax Credit and the Ontario Media Development Corporation.

Contents

1

Introduction

You can't please all the people all the time.

Nowhere is that free-floating internet maxim truer than when it comes to a work of art, with its baked-in subjectivity, its reliance on context and historical precedent, and its right-brained appeal to emotion and the senses. Storytelling itself is as old as it is diverse, with a palette containing everything from Homeric ballads to hashtag rap. Illustration is an equally tricky beast, capable of turning viewers off with something as innocent as the thickness of the artist's pen stroke. Mediums aside, creators must also stick their project's flag somewhere on the continuum between realism and abstraction, each with their attendant fans and detractors. And if, on top of all that, your art is meant to be *funny*? God help you. Most of the time, a joke broad enough for everyone to understand is by definition too bland for anyone whose taste veers toward the deep end of a particular niche or genre — and that's when the joke is successful. A vague, failed stab at comedy might be the most painful outcome of all.

And yet, even in our world of jumbled, almost hopelessly opposing tastes, sometimes the stars do align. Sometimes, you wind up with a comic strip like *Calvin and Hobbes*.

Created by Bill Watterson, and making its newspaper debut in 1985, *Calvin and Hobbes* is the story of a six-year-old boy and the stuffed tiger that, in Calvin's eyes, becomes his real-life (and occasionally feral) best friend. The strip is a blend of casual intelligence, rich characterization, visual panache, and noble goofery, and it ran in thousands of papers across North America from 1985 until its abrupt retirement ten years later. Since then, the strip has lived on in tens of millions of books, in dozens of different languages, all around the world. But most impressive of all is the fact that almost nobody seems to actively dislike it.

"I've never met anyone who doesn't like *Calvin and Hobbes*," Jenny Robb, curator of the Billy Ireland Cartoon Library and Museum, once said. "And I can't say that about any other strip."[1] During its run, *Calvin and Hobbes* quickly established itself as both a critical and commercial juggernaut. It won seven consecutive Harvey Awards for Best Syndicated Comic Strip, and by 1988, Watterson had become the youngest cartoonist, at age 30, to win the prestigious Reuben Award twice. Meanwhile, the strip routinely topped newspaper readers' polls, and its annual book collections each enjoyed first printings that ran into the seven figures. Even when you take this query to the internet at large, where hatred for any conceivable topic is always just a few keystrokes away, the lovefest continues. Aside from a single newspaper cartoonist who in the '90s once said that he never bought Watterson's premise, the closest I came was Google suggesting some alternate search terms. Did I perhaps mean "calvin and hobbes i hate when my boogers freeze"? (No, but now that you mention it . . .)

So how did Watterson do it? The secret to the strip's appeal was that it had multiple appeals. Watterson infused *Calvin and Hobbes* with a winning mix of high-minded philosophy and gross-out humor from the very beginning. One strip might feature Calvin looking to the sky, solemnly mulling over the meaning of life; in the next, he's wrestling a sentient bowl of oatmeal. Meanwhile, Hobbes — named after the 17th-century philosopher who had, as Watterson put it, "a dim view of human nature"[2] — was as likely to serve as the rational check on Calvin's harebrained schemes as he was the animal id, ready to pounce on his best friend the moment he got home from school. Watterson wasn't afraid to name-drop obscure French painters, or to write multi-day stories in which the majority of the characters are dinosaurs. And present in all of his work was a seemingly limitless sense of creativity. Watterson walked the line between reality and fantasy with uncommon agility, and he took even greater delight in smooshing the two realms together, showing all the ways his six-year-old hero could use his imagination as a refuge from a real world that was too oppressive, too literal-minded, and too flat-out boring to be tolerated for any significant length of time.

Calvin won readers over because he remains one of the most perfectly distilled visions of childhood ever committed to paper: rude, petulant, screamingly funny, gross, wise beyond his years, and utterly oblivious — sometimes all at the same time. In a strip about the threat and the promise of growing up, Calvin was our Peter Pan, allowed to remain young forever while we were forced away into the rank and file of adulthood. And his creator's decision to avoid topical references has allowed *Calvin and Hobbes* to live on, too, unscathed by the passage of time, as potent now as it ever was. While undeniably a product of his time and place (the American Midwest, circa 1985–1995), Calvin embodies the enduring nature of what it means to be six years old about as well as any fictional character ever has.

At the same time, Calvin's success as a character owes a lot to the larger universe he traveled within. *Calvin and Hobbes* has a cast of fewer than ten regular characters, and the majority of the strips take place in and around its protagonist's house. Yet the strip has enough imaginative firepower to suggest an almost infinite supply of people and ideas hiding around every corner — most of which came straight out of Calvin's almost uncontrollable imagination. Spaceman Spiff. Tracer Bullet. Stupendous Man. The transmogrifier. Calvinball. These weren't mere throwaway gags; rather, they were fully realized strips-within-the-strip, each with its own vocabulary, tone, and even visual style. And when Watterson *did* decide to reference something outside the world of the strip, it was always with the intention of surprising readers, pushing their curiosity into realms well beyond the funny pages.

Most comics are content to half-heartedly riff on the news stories covered elsewhere in that day's paper, but despite the medium's lowbrow reputation — or maybe because of it — Watterson strove to make his references as lofty as possible, shouting out Paul Gauguin or Karl Marx rather than whatever celebrity was making headlines that week. Even in his vocabulary, Watterson went above and beyond, sprinkling in exotic words and phrases like *avant garde*, *cognoscenti*, and *hara-kiri*. In one strip, Calvin asks Hobbes, "What if somebody calls us 'a pair o' pathetic peripatetics'?!" He adds, "Shouldn't we have a ready retort?"

Untold numbers of kids, newly galvanized as they read this strip over their morning cereal, banged their spoons on the table in agreement: *Shouldn't they?*

This is the part of the introduction where I neatly pivot into a long, meandering reminiscence about what *Calvin and Hobbes* meant to me as a kid, how it shaped and broadened my understanding of the world, and why the strip continues to take up more than its fair share of real estate in my head, all these years later.

I'll spare you all that. Not because it isn't true, but because I now know there wasn't anything particularly noteworthy about my experience with the strip. For a certain kind of kid in the late '80s and early '90s — reasonably intelligent, prone to daydreaming, alternately curious and skeptical about this adult world their parents gave them only occasional glimpses of — *Calvin and Hobbes* was a revelation. It was a strip about childhood, written in large part for children, that never condescended to them about it. Even if the people in Calvin's family didn't appreciate or respect the finer points of his inner life, Watterson always did. And despite Calvin being a middle-class white kid living in middle America, his interests and concerns were universal. Every kid who read the strip dreamed of having a best friend like Hobbes, and also saw a bit of themselves — maybe more than they'd like to admit — in Calvin. I was no different. Reading the strip felt like a secret message was being passed through the newspaper each morning, one that only I was able to decode. Perhaps the strip's greatest virtue was being able to forge that same personal connection with so many readers at once, all around the world. The effect *Calvin and Hobbes* had on me was significant on a personal level, and yet completely ordinary.

At the same time, that ordinariness is exactly why the strip matters: not because it hit home for one kid, but because it did so for millions of them. And for an entire generation of artists, writers, and other creative types, *Calvin and Hobbes* isn't just a reference point; it's part of their origin stories. Watterson's strip was one of the catalysts for their own journeys, following their imaginations into whatever weird, tiger-infested corners they could uncover.

That isn't to say that kids are perfect readers, of course. I certainly wasn't. For instance, while religiously reading and rereading those *Calvin and Hobbes* book collections, I had no inkling that, behind the scenes, Watterson was having a series of tense standoffs with his publishing syndicate about creative control — or that those grievances had actually worked themselves out onto the page. At the tail end of the strip's run, Watterson published *The Calvin and Hobbes Tenth Anniversary Book*, an annotated collection of his favorite stories from over the years. But it opens with a series of oddly prickly mini-essays about the perils of licensing, the restrictions of the newspaper format, and the decline of newspaper comics in general. I ran out to buy a copy, then flipped right past these sections, oblivious, in hot pursuit of the parts where Watterson talked about Calvinball. Only now, looking back, do I really see the creative churn going on in the background, which fueled many of the strip's greatest achievements and which ultimately led to its demise.

Again, that response is likely typical among my age group. Even though *Calvin and Hobbes* has always been a strip about the collision of fantasy and reality, mind and body, and, yes, even art and business, it still worked if all you wanted out of it were those silly drawings of treehouses and alien planets. After all, it was only Calvin's parents who were in favor of things like nutritious breakfasts and building character — and who in their right mind identified with Calvin's *parents*? Reading the *Tenth Anniversary Book* now, however, I have to admit that choosing between these opposing forces isn't as easy as it once was. (Calvin's dad has his charms, doesn't he?) Regardless of which camp you fall into, it's obvious in hindsight that the strip was powered by these kinds of tension, both on and off the page. It turned out that Watterson's work tended to improve whenever he was forced to work within restrictions: either the kind dictated by the newspaper format, or the constant pressures exerted by his publisher, who *really* hoped their star client could be convinced to give up a small amount of creative control in exchange for a line of plush Hobbes dolls and a bus full of cash. But Watterson could not be swayed. He had a vision, and he was going to stick to it, no matter the cost.

This is a book about imagination: its sources, its powers, and, ultimately, its limits. From the beginning, *Calvin and Hobbes* was built around the inner world of its six-year-old protagonist, and that spirit would define the strip for the next decade. Watterson expertly framed childhood as a tug of war between endless possibility and total lack of control. When Calvin is forced to interact with the people around him — his parents, his teacher, the girl next door — he comes off as aloof, scattered, gross. It's only when he is on his own, trudging through the forest behind his house, stuffed tiger in tow, that Calvin can truly be himself. This makes for a comic strip that is thrilling, hilarious, and impossible to predict, and yet one that is also tinged with a distant sense of sadness. Calvin's imagination is the saving grace that makes his childhood bearable. But he has no human friends to speak of, and very little in the way of an adult role model.

He is, deep down, a lonely kid. By using his mind as an endless internal playground, Calvin is able to keep that loneliness at bay and insulate himself from the real world around him. This act of imaginative cocooning is what gave the strip its bittersweet edge, and also what made it such a potent source of nostalgia for readers, especially as time went on. Because we had to grow up, and Calvin didn't. Each time we return to the strip changed, yet he will forever exist just below the horizon line of adulthood, unburdened by social norms, but also completely unaware of all that he's missing out on.

We'll begin by looking at the role of imagination in the strip itself, charting the progression of Calvin and Hobbes from minor characters in a totally different comic to the stars of one of the most beloved strips of its generation. Over the course of two chapters we'll consider the strip's meteoric rise, as well as its sudden, painful end. From there, we'll look at the way *C&H* fans have tried to use their own imaginations to fill the void the strip left behind — especially since Watterson himself has largely kept out of the public eye. Finally, we'll look at the strip's legacies, both accidental and intentional. Watterson's staunch refusal to merchandise the strip means that there have been no tie-in products to keep the strip alive in mainstream culture. And yet it lives on anyway: through the books; through a wide swath of tributes, imitations, and cameos in other creators' work; and through one bizarre — and bizarrely popular — bootleg industry.

Now grab a scarf, and hop on this sled. We've got some exploring to do.

2

Treasure Everywhere

Calvin and Hobbes existed as a typical comic strip for exactly three panels.

With the benefit of hindsight, we can now state definitively that over the course of the strip's ten-year run — more than 3,000 strips in all — Bill Watterson's creation would redefine the medium, in the process leaving a permanent wonder-scar on its readers that few other strips would ever match. When it comes to the title of the Last Great North American Comic Strip, there are no other serious contenders. In terms of critical acclaim, book sales, durability, influence on later strips, and even the basic ability to lasso an entire continent's worth of eyeballs every morning — unimaginable in the fractured 21st-century media landscape — Watterson stands alone. But even on that first day, November 18, 1985, in a quiet, four-panel debut in a handful of daily newspapers, there were already clues that this newcomer might have legs. Something was afoot.

In the first panel, we see a young boy in a pith helmet telling his father that he's off to check his tiger trap. The panel's framing puts the reader squarely in the shoes of the adult, who is washing the family car. The child is shown only from the neck up, as if stretching to get into the frame, while we can see that the father looks clean-cut and suburban, with a neat haircut, glasses, and a collared shirt with the sleeves rolled up. He has a blank look on his face, as if he's waiting to hear what this new game will require of him.

In the next panel, we pan down to get our first good look at the boy. He's as compressed as his dad is lanky, with a big, triangular smile, wearing a horizontally striped t-shirt and a smudge of dark pants, a pair of white sneakers poking out underneath. The boy is pounding his right fist into his left palm excitedly. He's proud of himself. See, he put a *tuna sandwich* in the trap.

In the third panel, we're back to the adult perspective. Dad now seems to have finished his internal risk assessment, and, satisfied that nothing disastrous is on the horizon, he turns back to the car. The boy, too, is already walking away.

So far, so good. We have an easily recognizable family dynamic between the kid with big dreams and the pragmatic father just trying to get through his chores. It's clear that these two are ships passing in the night, each with a head full of plans that do not overlap with each other's in the slightest. But in the strip's fourth and final panel, things go sideways. Now we cut straight past the kid, directly to his tiger trap, where *an actual tiger is there*, dangling upside-down with one ankle caught in a rope snare. But the tiger looks happy, too: he did get his sandwich, after all.

And . . . that's it. To be continued. See you tomorrow.

Any reader of this initial strip is bound to come away with a series of questions. What's going to happen when the boy gets back to the trap and sees he was successful? Is the tiger real? What's the boy hunting for — companionship, or a pelt? Which of these characters is Calvin? Is one of them Hobbes? And what is this strip *about*, anyway? Watterson's drawings are simple and evocative, but they leave out a lot of contextual information, most notably the backgrounds. A single tree branch in the final panel suggests the boy's trap was laid in the woods, and the presence of the car suggests the boy and his father are standing on the family driveway, but otherwise we have no hints of where we are, or where we go from here. The safari hat is a prop . . . right?

Many of these questions would, inevitably, get answered as the strip carried along. But others would be left intentionally up in the air. For instance, we learn that the boy is named Calvin. The tiger is Hobbes. And the general tone of the strip establishes itself soon afterward, with self-contained stories, set in the American Midwest, about bedtime arguments, the relative edibility of home-cooked meals, and monsters under the bed. But the biggest question from that initial story is only ever partly resolved. In the third-ever strip, Calvin's dad opens his son's bedroom door to tell him to stop making so much racket and go to sleep. Calvin leaps to his own defense, swearing that it was the stuffed tiger next to him who was actually making the noise. Dad isn't buying it. But he leaves the room anyway, and as soon as he does, something incredible happens between panels, a never fully explained transformation that would power the strip for the next decade: Hobbes is suddenly alive again, morphing from a lifeless toy back into the same walking, talking animal we saw snared in the trap on day one. Everything else in the scene is the same. Except now there's a giant cat in Calvin's bed, holding a pair of cymbals and protesting his innocence.

What happened between those two panels? Hobbes is obviously connected in some way to Calvin's mind, but how, exactly? Their relationship turns out to be more complex than it first appeared. One temptation is to see Hobbes as an object of actual magic, an ordinary doll whose true form is unlocked and released by the love of his owner — or, put another way, as an inherently magical creature who retreats into his inanimate shell whenever there are people other than Calvin around. (Kids prefer this explanation.) Another is to say that Hobbes is just a plain old doll, and that Calvin simply has an overactive imagination. (Adults tend to choose this one.) But to adopt this second viewpoint, you'd have to also admit that Calvin isn't *choosing* to see Hobbes this way; in fact, we'll see plenty of times throughout the strip where Calvin actively wishes Hobbes wasn't the larger-than-life feline that he appears to be. At the same time, the pure-magic hypothesis doesn't really hold up, either. Twice in the strip's first week alone, we see what appear to be two conflicting worldviews existing simultaneously: Calvin looks at Hobbes and sees his best friend in the world, and at the exact same time, another person looks at him and sees nothing but plush.

The question of Hobbes's "true" nature was built into the strip's appeal, but Watterson had no interest in resolving it off the page. "I hate to subject it to too much analysis," he said in an early interview.[3] "When Hobbes is a stuffed toy in one panel and alive in the next, I'm juxtaposing the 'grown-up' version of reality with Calvin's version, and inviting the reader to decide which is truer." Nobody would dispute that children and adults see the world in fundamentally different ways, arguing at cross-purposes to the point where they may as well be living in entirely different worlds. So is it really far-fetched that those differences in perspective could converge on a particular object? "The nature of Hobbes's reality doesn't interest me," Watterson re-affirmed years later, in the *Tenth Anniversary Book*, "and each story goes out of its way to avoid resolving the issue . . . Hobbes is more about the subjective nature of reality than about dolls coming to life."[4]

So there you have it: two subjective realities, coexisting, with no attempt to draw a clean line between them. Indeed, the strip would soon hit its stride poking around in the places where those realities disagreed, teasing out the gaps — between worldviews, as well as between the panels themselves — for comedic effect. And the key difference between those two realities? A surplus of imagination in Calvin's, and a frustrating lack of it in everyone else's.

Bill Watterson was born in the late 1950s and grew up in a small town on the outskirts of Cleveland called Chagrin Falls. Slightly ominous name notwithstanding, the town was in many ways picturesque, with a bustling Main Street full of mom-and-pop stores, stately Victorian architecture, a town triangle complete with bandstand, a natural waterfall, and some sprawling woods at the edge of town that became a *de facto* playground for the local kids. In Watterson's words: "Very Norman Rockwell — all white, very Republican."[5] But the town's blue-collar origins were never far away, either. Chagrin Falls began life as a mill town, and as a kid, Watterson used to watch the river turn red from the dye that the local paper-bag factory would dump straight into the water.

An eager artist from a young age, self-taught by countless dinosaur and bird drawings, Watterson was also a lifelong comics fan. He grew up a devotee of Charles Schulz's *Peanuts*, reading the strip the way many kids do: giggling at Snoopy the fighter pilot, and not really processing — consciously, anyway — the strip's deeper emotional subtleties. Then, in middle school, Watterson picked up a collection of Walt Kelly's *Pogo* strips at a library book sale. It was meant to be a gift for his dad, but Watterson ended up keeping the collection for himself — even if at the time he wasn't quite sure why. "The cartoons were so dense and black," he remembered later, "with a thousand words in every strip. It was a visually oppressive thing to look at when you've grown up on *Peanuts*."[6] Even at a young age, for Watterson these two comics became the mental goalposts that *Calvin and Hobbes* would later try to shoot between:

he loved the way Kelly's humor derived from actual dialogue, as opposed to stiff punchlines, while Schulz's "economy of line," he said, "perfectly suited my lack of patience."[7] (A third creative totem, George Herriman's *Krazy Kat*, would arrive later in life.) In Chagrin Falls, Watterson also read Batman comics, and *Mad* magazine, and pretty much any other cartoons he could get his hands on. But nothing else made the same kind of impression.

By the time he was a teenager, Watterson had become a relentless scribbler and doodler. From homemade cards and posters to the margins of his homework, Watterson "hardly let a sheet of paper get by me without putting a cartoon on it."[8] He drew illustrations for his high school's newspaper and yearbook, and he got editorial cartoons published in his local newspaper, the *Sun Herald*, even before graduating. One memorable example of the latter was a response to the town purchasing some fancy new police cruisers. With his mother's encouragement, Watterson whipped up an exaggerated drawing of "a souped-up police car with all sorts of bells, whistles, and foghorns on top."[9] The paper was so pleased, they didn't just run the cartoon — they *enlarged* it.

From there, Watterson was on to the renowned liberal-arts school Kenyon College, a few hours downstate. At Kenyon, he mucked around for a while in the English department before eventually majoring in political science after being seduced by some unusually high-quality political cartoons he saw in the student paper. These, it turned out, were drawn by Jim Borgman, a whiz kid who had just graduated and been immediately hired by the *Cincinnati Enquirer*. Seeing what appeared to be a straightforward career path in front of him, Watterson, too, tried to go the editorial cartoon route, despite having little knowledge of local government, politics, or even the news in general. "I see now that this was rather a liability," Watterson deadpanned later, "but ignorance breeds courage."[10] Mostly he used his college education as an opportunity to get a grounding in the classics, but he didn't find much inspiration in the likes of Machiavelli, Plato, and Hobbes — other than a useful character name to be squirreled away for later. Undeterred, Watterson drew weekly comics in the college newspaper throughout his tenure at Kenyon, cobbled together a portfolio, and went out looking for work.

He ended up finding more than he bargained for. Watterson was lucky enough to land a job with another major daily in nearby Cincinnati, the *Post* — which meant that he would be in direct competition with the *Enquirer* and Jim Borgman, the wunderkind who'd inspired him to venture into the field in the first place. (Borgman would go on to win a Pulitzer Prize for his cartoons, and would later co-create the teen comic strip *Zits*, which appears in more than 1,700 newspapers worldwide.) Watterson immediately floundered in the pressures of a daily newsroom. He struggled to generate ideas, and by his own admission, he didn't understand the local political landscape enough to lampoon it effectively. Very little of what he did pitch ever made it onto the page. Halfway into his six-month stint, Watterson's editor even gave him the option of walking away, no harm, no foul. But Watterson had rent to pay. So he stuck around, and floundered some more.

Once the newspaper contract mercifully ran out, Watterson moved back in with his parents and tried to re-imagine what a career in cartooning might look like. From 1981 to 1985, he worked a demoralizing day job laying out ads for a free shopping newspaper, took whatever freelance illustration gigs came his way — which ranged from one-off t-shirt designs to a series of drawings for a literary journal about Mark Twain — and tried to drum up ideas for original comic strips in whatever free time was left over. There wasn't a lot of method to Watterson's madness, though. "These [strips] were random shots in the dark," he said.[11] Again, Watterson had raw talent, but not much business acumen; he didn't really know how the world of newspaper syndicates worked, and he spent years trying to guess at what their editors wanted, rather than following any of his own creative impulses, which would inevitably lead to richer and better material. Strips about animals, college students, high-strung newspaper reporters (this one might have had a grain of autobiography to it), and intergalactic hijinks were all duly sent up the flagpole and then sent right back down again. "What I didn't realize was that nobody out there knows what they're looking for until they see it," he said later. "You don't build the peg to fit a hole; the peg needs to bore its own hole."[12]

Watterson may not have had any fully formed strip ideas lying around, but he did have a couple of spare parts that might be able to be repurposed. The first was a character who'd been showing up in his sketchbooks since high school, when Watterson first drew a crude two-page strip about a smoking,

18

mustachioed astronaut named Raumfahrer Rolf for an assignment in German class. The character popped up again in the pages of the Kenyon College newspaper as Spaceman Mort, and was revamped yet again as Spaceman Spiff, hero of the very first strip Watterson submitted to the syndicates. The other character destined for a second chance was a peripheral figure in another strip Watterson had tried to sell, without success. An editor at United Features told Watterson they were passing on the main idea. *But what about that kid — the one with the stuffed tiger that comes to life? Do you think there might be something there?*

All of a sudden, things started to click. Watterson, who had initially shied away from writing a strip built around kids, for fear that he'd be ripping off his idol Schulz, found that he was easily able to channel some of his own childhood into his precocious protagonist, and the dynamic between the boy and his tiger quickly opened up new possibilities for silliness on the page. "There's a lack of literalness when you work with those kinds of characters that I found very freeing," he said later. "Readers just naturally cut kids and animals more slack." Most importantly, however, the strip finally had its own distinct voice — that hard-to-define, harder-to-bottle X factor that had eluded Watterson for years. Now that he'd found a voice, he wasn't going to let it go. "When you get that," he said, "you grab on tight."[13]

There were a few more bumps on the way to publication. Sarah Gillespie, the editor at United Features who had first spotted the Calvin character — then named Marvin — turned out to be unable to sell the strip to her superiors, thanks in part to some disappointing focus-group results. "United didn't take *Calvin and Hobbes* because a couple housewives in Connecticut said, 'It's OK, but we don't get it,'" she told author Nevin Martell.[14] Thus, Watterson found himself back at square one. The rejection stung, to be sure. But this time he knew he had something, and it wasn't long afterward that a different group, Universal Press Syndicate, took on the strip and gave him the final green light.

But Watterson also had to make some aesthetic changes. It's difficult to imagine now, but the Calvin character originally had long bangs that covered half of his face, until it was pointed out to Watterson that readers might have an easier time identifying with the strip's main character if they could see his eyes. So, at the last minute, Watterson revised the best of his sample strips and prepared (along with his editors, Jake Morrissey and Lee Salem) sales kits for prospective newspaper editors across the country, and *Calvin and Hobbes* made its humble debut in 35 North American funny pages that fall.

Watterson was thrilled, but Salem warned him not to quit his day job just yet. Getting a strip accepted, he told him, was the easy part. Now the real work would begin.

Few creative fields are as strict and unforgiving as the daily comic strip. You've got a limited space to work with, the exact scale and placement of which on the page is completely out of your control. Plus, your work needs to appeal to that mythical figure, the "average newspaper reader," of whom little is known except that she is easily offended, resistant to change, and extremely fickle. You also don't have color to work with, except on Sundays — but then again, those strips need to be prepared months in advance, so they almost never tie in to what's going on in the rest of the strip anyway. The average weekday strip gives you at most four panels in which to generate a joke, and you have to constantly balance that humor quota with the larger tasks of building a world, a cast of characters, and, ultimately, a body of work that is, with any luck, more than just the sum of its parts. Oh yeah, and you need to come up with a new one of these things *every day*. Then, once you manage to find your legs, the best-case scenario is to keep this routine up, seven days per week, until you die — at which point your assistant or children will pick up your pen and try to carry on in your stead.

When *Calvin and Hobbes* launched, Watterson wasn't quite scrambling to stay afloat. For one thing, he had a cushion of all the material he'd already written and inked as part of his submissions to the syndicate. He also likely enjoyed the freedom and exhilaration that comes with handling any creative project in its infancy. The parameters of the strip hadn't yet been defined, so anything was possible. At the same time, in fleshing out Calvin's world, every subsequent decision Watterson made would quietly seal off other, unrealized storylines and approaches; if it was revealed early on that, say, Calvin lived in a single detached home (as he did), then it would stand to reason that he couldn't live in a shiny downtown condo, or on a dairy farm, or on a boat. This gradual narrowing effect applied to everything from simple aesthetics (should the strip be drawn with brushes or pens?), to storytelling devices (is there a narrator?), to chronology (do the characters age?). If he isn't careful in how he goes about world-building, a creator can paint himself into a corner very early on, and then have to live with those consequences for years to come.

Which makes it all the more impressive that Watterson was able to avoid such traps, either by design or, more likely, by some impressive good luck. Consider this: the central cast of *Calvin and Hobbes* is all established in the first three weeks. In week one, we meet Calvin, Hobbes, and Calvin's (otherwise unnamed) dad, plus we get a cameo from his elderly teacher, Miss Wormwood — not as curmudgeonly as she'll later become, but drawn identically, with a polka-dot dress, square-framed glasses, and short curls on top. In week two, we meet Calvin's (also unnamed) mom, and in week three, eternal nemesis/crush Susie Derkins moves in down the street. Give or take a school bully and a babysitter, Watterson wouldn't introduce another major character for the next 3,000 strips.

As it turns out, he wouldn't need to. The reason *Calvin and Hobbes* was able to maintain its skeleton crew of characters is because from the beginning, Watterson was an expert at making the world of the strip feel much larger, and more populated, than it really was. Again, this comes back to the idea of imagination. Why would Calvin even need flesh-and-blood people in his life when he's always a few seconds away from flying to Mars on his wagon or building his latest postmodern masterpiece out of snow? It's no accident that the first strip shows him discovering a feline best friend way out in the forest, away from civilization. Actual humans that Calvin can relate to will always be in short supply.

Watterson was as pleased by this development as anyone. "In a way, it's surprised me that the strip hasn't exhausted its cast very much at all," he told *The Comics Journal* in 1989.[15] "The babysitter came after a few months but, really, aside from that, the strip has stayed the same as I originally planned it." In fact, Watterson wasn't sure he would be able to wholly avoid the trap of introducing new characters to freshen things up. But he hoped to restrict himself to the occasional minor figure or two. "I don't expect to add a major character into the center of the strip," he said. "The strip's world is a very small insulated one, which, I think, is more natural to me."

The content of these early strips, too, is almost wholly built around Calvin's runaway imagination and the various adults in his life attempting to manage it. Hobbes holding the cymbals set the theme. But the next day, Calvin brings Hobbes to school, and freaks out when he's told — nicely, to Miss Wormwood's credit — that his tiger doll needs to be put away. "In my locker?!" Calvin replies, aghast. "He'll suffocate!" Several other early stories revolve around monsters living under Calvin's bed. We never see any outright, but Calvin is a pro at tricking them into revealing their existence. In the first-ever Sunday strip, Calvin and Hobbes work themselves into such a post-bedtime panic that they arm themselves with horns and dart guns, then go ballistic on the green monstrosity that bursts into the bedroom.

Only in the last panel does the perspective flip, and we now see Calvin's dad, back in the hallway, unamused and covered with suction-cup arrows. Elsewhere, Calvin battles a murderous, human-shaped pile of bath bubbles and turns every innocent game playing with sand castles or toy trucks into a complex, high-stakes disaster movie. (After setting a sports car, a cement truck, and a chemical truck speeding toward one another, he turns to address the reader directly, making us his other secret confidante: "This ought to be good.") He can't even try an unfamiliar dinner food without imagining it's a steaming pile of bat vomit. And all of these different scenarios take place in the same mundane settings of Calvin's home and school. The early days of the strip operated as a kind of challenge: if he could fuel a month's worth of material from this one premise, how much further could Watterson take it?

Spaceman Spiff would also make three appearances before the end of that first calendar year, taking readers from the depths of intergalactic torture chambers to "megazorks above Planet Gloob" (in reality, the principal's office and the top of the playground slide, respectively). Characters like Spiff offered Watterson an easy way out. For one thing, much of the material was readymade, having already spent years marinating in his sketchbooks and previous syndicate submissions. Plus, as an alter-ego who lives several galaxies away from the strip's home planet, Spiff and his space-trotting adventures didn't use up any of the finite material in Calvin's everyday life, instead giving him a parallel, fully formed alternate realm to play around in. By Watterson's own admission, these stories gave him a chance "to draw some other comic strip" — one that was full of exotic alien landscapes and comically specific blaster-ray technology — "when I want[ed] a break from *Calvin and Hobbes*."[16] Spiff's world was constantly expanding, too, with Watterson never content to reuse the gibberish name of a far-flung planet or alien slimeball when he could think up a new one instead.

Practically, the Spaceman Spiff strips, which gleefully borrowed from pulp sci-fi like *Flash Gordon* and also drew on Watterson's childhood fascination with the Apollo moon program, were Calvin's go-to defense mechanism against the boredom of school, and they operated on a simple but winning formula. Each strip opens with the reader fully immersed in Spiff's world, with some kind of high-stakes battle or chase scene already underway. Spiff, who looks basically the same as Calvin, except clad in a futuristic jumpsuit and wearing a large black visor over his eyes, then uses his cunning and daredevilry to try to get out of harm's way — until the last panel suddenly cuts back to the classroom, and we see the consequences of Calvin's fantasy spilling over into the real world. Usually this results in a trip to the principal's office, but sometimes his flights of fancy accidentally pay off. In one strip, Susie whispers to a daydreaming Calvin for help with a question on their history test. He answers, "Krakow! Krakow!" — which is the sound Spiff's blasters make in his fantasy world, but also happens to be the correct answer to "the capital of Poland until 1600."*

---

* Technically 1596, but considering it's a class of first-graders, that's got to be worth at least half marks.

It's hard to say whether Watterson's previous incarnations of Spiff would have been as successful on their own terms, because the key to Calvin's Spiff is the juxtaposition between this dashing, brave space adventurer, completely in control of his own destiny, and the six-year-old boy who can't even go to the bathroom without asking permission. Spiff is a figure of pure wish fulfillment, and Calvin's constant use of this fantasy neatly demonstrates the distance between a kid's inner life and the one he lets everyone else see. This might explain why Watterson uses the Spiff character more often than any of the strip's other recurring fantasy devices — 16 times in the first year alone. But the parallel-universes conceit clearly worked, and in future years Watterson would try it again, using different genres as the springboard: first the noir detective Tracer Bullet, who showed up whenever Calvin's mom rhetorically asked him who broke something in the house, and later, the superhero Stupendous Man.

Of the two, the Tracer Bullet stories provided the clearest gap between fantasy and reality. Watterson drew these strips in a darker, more cluttered style, full of long shadows cast by venetian blinds and ominous trails of cigarette and/or pistol smoke. The character originated when Calvin was forced to wear a vaguely detective-looking hat after Hobbes gave him an unflattering haircut, but, like Spiff, he stuck around because he was able to refract Calvin's point of view through a genre lens. He wasn't bad with a tossed-off Chandlerism, either. "I keep two magnums in my desk," Bullet says in one strip. "One's a gun, and I keep it loaded. The other's a bottle, and it keeps *me* loaded." The storytelling possibilities that came with having a new vocabulary and visual style to play around with were just icing on the cake. The main thing Bullet's world had in common with Calvin's, however, was its overarching sense of injustice and corruption: each adventure finished with Bullet realizing he'd been set up to take the fall for the crime, because of course Calvin had been, too.

Stupendous Man was a more commonly deployed, but ultimately less successful, alter-ego. A self-billed "champion of liberty, defender of free will," this character straddled the line between fantasy and reality in ways that Spiff and Bullet never did. On the one hand, Stupendous Man was powerful enough to reverse the earth's orbit to prolong the weekend, while on the other, Calvin really did walk around wearing the hood and cape (which his mom made for him). So it wasn't always clear where Stupendous Man's world ended and Calvin's began. At the same time, the exaggerated language of comic books wasn't that far off from a standard *Calvin and Hobbes* strip, especially the lively *kapows!* and *whams!* that accompanied Hobbes every time he pounced on Calvin walking in the front door from school. It made sense that Calvin, an inveterate comic book nut, would try to emulate the world of biceps and spandex, but Stupendous Man didn't show readers anything they didn't already know.

If characters like Spaceman Spiff and Tracer Bullet allowed Calvin to imagine himself as the hero of an alternate universe, he was equally drawn to fantasies where he could loom above and play god instead. In one early strip, Calvin spends two panels narrating a story about a city he's building in the sandbox, only to then rush over to the tap at the side of his house, fill up a bucket, and announce: "Tragically, this serene metropolis lies directly beneath the Hoover Dam . . ." A later Sunday strip devotes ten full panels to the twists and turns of a game Calvin is playing with a miniature car driving along the edge of the couch. After poor "Mr. Jones" speeds along next to the Grand Canyon, careens over the side, and gets blown to bits when his car explodes in midair, Calvin sits, silent, for a single panel before getting bored, picking the car back up, and imagining the neighbors going over to investigate. This god complex of his is made explicit in another strip wherein Calvin imagines himself as a literal deity, complete with flowing beard, surrounded by the swirling cosmos as he builds and destroys worlds on a whim. (In reality, he's playing with a Tinkertoys set in the living room.) It's tempting to read these strips as Calvin's morbid take on innocent childhood pastimes — something that Calvin himself encourages by referring to himself as an Old Testament kind of god, demanding sacrifice and causing unnecessary pain — but, really, isn't he doing what every kid does, subverting a toy's supposed function and wringing something new from it? Sure, Calvin's turbo-charged imagination gives his games a level of detail that goes above and beyond what your typical six-year-old might come up with, but moments like these remind us of the universality of childhood that Calvin so often taps into. And by playing god, sometimes literally, he's able to retain a level of control over his adventures that even Spiff cannot.

Fantasy shows up in *Calvin and Hobbes* in a variety of ways. On one end of the spectrum, we have fully immersive alternate worlds, like Spaceman Spiff's, where for large chunks of time we are essentially reading a different comic strip, the joke arriving at the very last minute as readers — and Calvin himself — suddenly crash back to reality. And on the other end, we have the toy car gags, where readers hear Calvin narrate an outlandish scenario while seeing him the way any adult might: from a distance, always aware that the scene he's describing is entirely in his head. More often, however, Watterson tries to split the difference. Perhaps the single most common premise in the strip involves Calvin imagining one part of his real world suddenly transformed. Usually it's Calvin himself doing the changing: into an octopus or a frog, a living x-ray, a puddle of water, or a particle of light. At different times, he imagines that he has for some reason become very small, or — over the course of a few surreal weeks — is growing steadily larger, dwarfing his house and eventually the entire galaxy. He imagines he is a new kind of super-powerful "C-Bomb." He imagines he is a volcano. And a hummingbird. And one of his own crude drawings come to life. And, most often of all — dozens of times over the course of the strip — a dinosaur, doing everything from devouring kids on the playground to nesting in the pantry. These self-contained strips again follow the Spiff template, with the reader dropped into a Kafkaesque world out of nowhere, and Calvin self-narrating his quest to understand what's happened to him. This continues for a couple of panels, until the last one pulls back to reveal the effect Calvin's real-world commitment to his fantasy is having on the people around him: the hummingbird is really just Calvin guzzling pop, the x-ray merely him chewing with his mouth open at the dinner table. But these bystanders aren't privy to the scope and scale of Calvin's fantasies, so they aren't sympathetic to the part of the performance they *can* see. Why would they be? Calvin's fantasy world is, at heart, a coping mechanism against a world that he wants no part of. As a six-year-old with no control over the vast majority of his day-to-day life, he constantly finds himself in situations and around people that he would never choose of his own volition. One particularly brutal Sunday strip from 1989 makes this abundantly clear. We follow Calvin as he is dragged through a series of unwanted situations: his mom yells at him for oversleeping, his teacher publically embarrasses him for blanking on a math question, his dad tells him to eat his radioactive dinner faster, he's steered away from toys and TV toward the bathtub and then bed — where his mom kisses him on the head and says, "Have a good night's sleep. Tomorrow's another big day!" The last panel shows Calvin still awake, in the middle of the night, sighing inconsolably. Watterson was skilled at finding the humor in childhood, but this strip is so depressing, and so realistic, that it is actually hard to read. Later, it was included in the *Tenth Anniversary Book* with plain commentary from the cartoonist: "I've never understood people who remember childhood as an idyllic time."[17] Like a lot of kids, Calvin's only escape from the drudgery of everyday life is through fantasy, and its total absence in this strip — even his trusty Hobbes isn't there — only reinforces how deeply he relies on it, and how utterly lost he is without it.

Fortunately, as an only child who is given virtually limitless unsupervised playtime by his parents, Calvin has no shortage of nooks and crannies in which to hunker down, open up the floodgates, and let his imagination take over. The bus stop inspires certain kinds of fantasies, which are more pessimistic and dystopian than those generated by the woods behind his house, which in turn are more freeing and expansive than those associated with the bathtub upstairs. Watterson never provided any kind of definitive topographic map to the places Calvin and Hobbes hung out in, but dedicated readers of the strip likely came up with their own informal versions anyway.

In fact, I would argue that Watterson's true genius — the thing that keeps *Calvin and Hobbes* feeling fresh and vital, all these years later — was his ability to leave certain areas unexplored and therefore unresolved. Even once the basic parameters of the strip were defined, there were always blank spots on the map that drove readers forward and left them genuinely unsure where a given story might wind up. Not only that, but the possibilities created by a given gap were always far more numerous than the single, actual detail omitted, thus creating an imaginative space that infinitely dwarfed the reality around it. Call it the trapdoor effect. And once you start noticing it, you'll see it everywhere.

We've already seen it in Hobbes's ability to be both a stuffed animal and a living tiger at the exact same moment. But it carries over into many other parts of the strip. Take something like *Hamster Huey and the Gooey Kablooie* (Calvin's favorite bedtime story), or the Noodle Incident (a particularly disastrous episode from school), two recurring gags in the strip that are never fully shown or explained. Withholding information like this is a fairly simple method of generating suspense, but Watterson stretches out the tension for years with no intention of it ever paying off. This way, whenever readers come across Calvin demanding that his dad read him *Hamster Huey* for the *nth* time, we know right away what kind of strip we're reading, yet we are still propelled by the promise of a crucial piece of information that, it turns out, was never forthcoming to begin with. This lack of closure could be frustrating for some readers — lack of closure in general became an issue for many *Calvin and Hobbes* fans, as we'll see later — but it also helped maintain an air of intrigue around the strip, as if the answers could be found if only we reread the collections with an even closer eye this time. As Calvin put it, *There's treasure everywhere*. When in doubt, keep digging.

The trapdoor effect is present in a lot of *Calvin and Hobbes*, but there are two recurring premises that capture its essence. The first isn't so much a single premise as it is a series of different stories woven throughout the fabric of the strip, variations on the same fantastic theme, the exact details of which depend on which way an oversized box is facing. First introduced in March 1987, Calvin's cardboard box is one of the strip's quintessential devices, a fan favorite that was guaranteed to push the strip into new and unfamiliar territory while merrily blurring the line between fantasy and reality with each new iteration. In the strip's first five years, Watterson used the cardboard box on ten separate occasions, most of which involved a multi-part storyline that spanned multiple weeks in the newspaper.

The basic idea is one that's patently obvious to any six-year-old: climb into the box, and something magical will happen. In Calvin's case, when the cardboard box is placed on the ground right side up, it's a time machine. On its side, it becomes a duplicator. And upside down, the box can either be a "Cerebral Enhance-O-Tron" (which does pretty much what it sounds like) or a transmogrifier, capable of turning whoever crawls inside it into something else entirely. Again, the key is that the box is designed to be an inexhaustible premise, with seemingly infinite potential uses. When Calvin first builds the transmogrifier, he makes this explicit by showing Hobbes the hand-drawn dial he's put on the side, which "automatically restructures your chemical configuration" into either an eel, a baboon, a giant bug, or a dinosaur. Hobbes asks what happens if you want to be something else. Calvin replies, "I left some room. Just write it on the side." Even though Calvin takes a relatively safe route, opting to become a tiger like his best friend, the lingering effect is irresistible: he could've become anything he wanted. And, more importantly, the box's already-miraculous properties can be reimagined with the stroke of a pen.

The cardboard box strips neatly capture the wide-ranging imaginative trawling that all kids of Calvin's age naturally excel at. But the way Watterson frames them, with the feeling that limitless possibilities are quite literally at the push of a button (or the writing of a single phrase), also taps into larger literary traditions. The Argentine short story writer Jorge Luis Borges knew firsthand the powers of infinity. Many of his stories are built around concepts like a never-ending library, but in one essay, Borges creates a taxonomy that sounds like exactly the kind of thing Calvin would adore. According to a (fictitious) Chinese encyclopedia, Borges writes, all animals can be divided into the following categories: "(a) those that belong to the Emperor, (b) embalmed ones, (c) those that are trained, (d) suckling pigs, (e) mermaids, (f) fabulous ones, (g) stray dogs, (h) those that are included in this classification, (i) those that tremble as if they were mad, (j) innumerable ones, (k) those drawn with a very fine camel's hair brush, (l) others, (m) those that have just broken a flower vase, (n) those that resemble flies from a distance."[18] Such a list gleefully undercuts any notion of order, and it's that "others" category, which isn't even listed at the end as a miscellaneous catchall, that sounds most Calvinian in its embrace of fantasy and imagination. *Just write it on the side.*

In fact, the initial transmogrifier story is fairly tame in terms of its willingness to push its premise to the breaking point. Calvin turns into a tiger, briefly confuses his parents (who of course can't see the extreme molecular rearrangement he's just undergone), and then transforms back again. Coming just 18 months into the strip's existence, Watterson was still testing the borders of what he could get away with in the daily funny pages. But he grew bolder with each new instalment of the cardboard box, not just changing and expanding its powers, but also stretching the stories themselves out further and further. Following the initial transmogrifier adventure (11 parts), Calvin would travel back to the Jurassic period (11 parts); accidentally create six duplicates of himself, only one of which had to go to school on a given day (22 parts); transform into an elephant, the better to memorize his homework; *return* to the Jurassic, this time to take photographs of dinosaurs that he could then sell for a fortune in the present day (12 parts); and re-duplicate himself, this time creating a clone only of his good side (15 parts). Elsewhere, Calvin would even streamline the technology to the point where the box itself was no longer necessary, replaced with a point-and-shoot transmogrifier gun (13 parts). "Calvin's transmogrifier sums up the spirit of the strip," Watterson agreed in the *Tenth Anniversary Book*. "A cardboard box becomes a series of great inventions with a little imagination. The transmogrifier shows the kind of kid Calvin is, and it added a new dimension to the strip's world."[19] As the strip grew, so too did the cardboard box stories, with Watterson not just searching for fresh premises, but also pushing at the outer edges of the strip's universe. After all, what is a comic strip but a series of boxes where magic sometimes happens?

Watterson has claimed that he never wrote stories with a particular ending in mind, so it is likely that the *other* recurring premise that captures the essence of the trapdoor effect — and the strip in general — came about entirely by accident. And it all began with Calvin's relationship with sports.

Just like in the classroom — where a sense of rule-bound claustrophobia leads him to imaginatively lash out — with sports Calvin finds himself once again in social situations governed by a series of dense, impenetrable rules that other kids seem to grasp intuitively. Worse, sports are supposed to be *fun*. And because they're often played during recess, what's meant to be a break from school becomes, for him, a perverse extension of it.

One particular storyline showcases Calvin's utter failure to grasp the entertainment value of a group sport like baseball. This story, which ran in the papers from April 16 to May 5, 1990, opens optimistically, with Calvin running outside at recess to discover a much-coveted free swing on the swing set. His good fortune, however, soon gives way to suspicion, since it isn't just one swing that's available, but all of them. What gives? A wandering-by Susie Derkins lets Calvin in on the awkward truth: the other boys at school — literally every single one of them — have signed up to play baseball. This is Calvin's nightmare, for several reasons. First is the obvious social stigma, as his rejection of a traditionally male activity is now made glaringly public. The second reason might be even worse: for the first time, Calvin has free rein of the playground, but he's unable to enjoy any of it, thanks to the looming flak he knows he's about to catch from the other boys. As it happens, the exclusive presence of girls isn't exactly a relief to him, either. Calvin's first response to Susie is to cover his mouth with his t-shirt and start yelling about how he hasn't been vaccinated against cooties yet.

Despite his theatrics, the depth of Calvin's social gaffe isn't immediately clear to him. He spends the next strip quietly playing with Susie on the teeter-totter, talking about his predicament to a rare sympathetic ear. "I'd rather just run around," he says. In organized sports, "Somebody's always yelling at you, telling you where to be, what to do, and when to do it." Calvin figures when he's ready to do that, he'll just join the army — because at least there you get paid. Too late: in the very next strip, Calvin gets ambushed at his locker by Moe, the school's resident bully. Word has gotten around about Calvin's supposedly sissy behavior. To avoid dragging out his (even more pronounced than usual) ostracization, Calvin slinks to the gym teacher's office and begrudgingly signs up to play.

Except, to him, it isn't really play at all. That night, Calvin complains to Hobbes about the rigidity of the way baseball is played at school. "This will be with *teams* and assigned positions and an umpire!" he says. "It's *boring* playing it the *real* way!" The implication is that Calvin has his own customized version of baseball that he won't share with his classmates — maybe because he's been burned before, or maybe because he knows they can't be convinced to try anything out of the ordinary. Hobbes asks whether he even knows how to play the real way, and once again we see a clear divide between Calvin in his natural freewheeling state and the socially acceptable poses he has to contort himself into whenever he's forced to engage with other people. "See, that's *another* problem!" Calvin replies. "Suppose they make me a halfback. Can I tackle the shortstop or not?"

From here, a series of events unfolds as a consequence of Calvin giving in to peer pressure, each somehow worse than the last. His dad offers to practice with him after dinner and ends up drilling a ground ball into an unsuspecting Calvin's nose. The next day, during his first game at school, Calvin is sent so far out into left field that he doesn't realize the teams have switched places mid-inning, and he ends up catching a fly ball, to his shock and delight — only to realize it was against his own batter. And when he finally pulls the plug on the whole experiment, he's branded a quitter by his teammates and coach alike. He just can't win. There's even a moment of direct imaginative conflict, as the fly ball Calvin catches also happens to interrupt one of his intergalactic Spaceman Spiff daydreams, which he's indulging in while standing by himself, so far in the outfield that he has to squint to see home plate; true fun is thus spoiled by its socially mandated derivative. Not only does Calvin fail the macho gauntlet put in front of him, but he also trips on every possible hurdle along the way.

This whole storyline, which includes many jokes over the span of its three weeks, has an undeniably cruel edge to it, not least of all because several other characters believe that Calvin's misadventure, while unnatural to a kid of his disposition, is also a necessary one. When his dad tries to give him his standard line about how sports, like everything else unpleasant in life, builds character, Calvin bristles even harder than usual. "What's wrong with just having fun by yourself, huh?!" he asks. Dad's reply, while staring meaningfully at the necktie he's just taken off: "When you grow up, it's not allowed." Later, at the bus stop, Calvin complains that girls never have to deal with this kind of aggro intimidation from their peers. Susie, again, is sympathetic to a point, but she points out that boys "aren't expected to spend their lives 20 pounds underweight." By then, however, Calvin isn't listening anymore; he's already thinking about all the beer commercials he'll never get to act in as a non-athlete. Another missed opportunity.

Watterson would draw on the world of baseball at other times in the strip. Whenever he did, the same basic tensions between fun based on rules and fun generated by chaos were always present — but as long as it was just Calvin and Hobbes doing the playing, these were resolved easily enough. Left to its own devices, imagination would always win out over the rule book. One such homespun "sport" includes at least 23 different bases, scattered around the backyard and surrounding forest area, that runners have to touch (and that's not counting the secret base). Another features a team of ghost players, whose invisible antics inevitably lead to a bench-clearing brawl. In these games, the baseball itself might become sentient and chase Calvin around his house or up into a tree. And in the wintertime, the snowy conditions are no impediment, either: just add a sled and a stockpile of snowballs, and you've got yourself a rousing game of "speed sled base snow ball," which, I mean, your guess is as good as mine, really.

The key, in all of these off-the-cuff games, is imagination — but a particular form of it, and always within certain parameters: not throwing the rules completely out the window, but rather adopting a constantly evolving rule book where pretty much anything is up for grabs. Any successful game, after all, requires enough formal structure to stay coherent and not just collapse into anarchy. And it's precisely that sense of controlled chaos that gives this story, where we see Calvin's imaginative potential stifled in a particularly painful and humiliating way, its silver lining.

Enter: Calvinball.

The baseball storyline concludes, fittingly, on a weekend, when the dual obligations of school and, now, the damned-if-he-does, damned-if-he-doesn't baseball team have faded away with the rest of the week. Disillusioned, Calvin wanders outside as Hobbes asks him what he wants to do. "Anything but play an organized sport," he replies. Hobbes scratches his head, then asks, "Want to play Calvinball?"

"YEAH!"

The final panel cuts to our first glimpse of this new and unfamiliar game. We're *in medias res*, and the scene is intentionally convoluted. Hobbes is carrying a polka-dot flag tied to a stick and fleeing from Calvin, who's in hot pursuit and aiming a soccer ball at his head. Both are dodging a series of numbered signs and croquet wickets set up haphazardly throughout the yard; both are also wearing dark bandanas over their eyes with holes cut out to see through. Most important, however, is that Calvin is announcing a rule change on the fly, wherein the unlucky player now has to hop around on one foot. This game, with its relentless creativity and its barely contained sense of chaos, would come to be one of the strip's most popular ideas, but its first appearance was nothing more than a throwaway joke, as Hobbes's final line makes clear: "No sport is less organized than Calvinball!"

Why did Calvinball capture the attention of so many readers? Watterson would bring it back on multiple occasions, and it was a fan favorite every time. But even in its first incarnation, he grasped its appeal immediately. "People have asked how to play Calvinball," Watterson wrote in the *Tenth Anniversary Book*. "It's pretty simple: you make up the rules as you go."[20] (Or here's Calvin, again addressing the reader directly: "The only permanent rule is that you can't play it the same way twice!")

To read a Calvinball strip is to feel as though you're in the eye of a hurricane that's about to engulf you. The game promises to deliver on the feeling of adventure promised by organized sports, but multiplied exponentially, and without any of that pesky *organized* part. Calvinball is also, crucially, a mongrel sport, grabbing rules, ideas, and bits of equipment from whatever other games may be lying around. This is a key source of its ramshackle charm, and one that has misled many a reader over the years into believing that they, too, could play a quick round or two once they fished a couple of rakes and badminton rackets out of the garage.

Alas, it's an illusion. In fact, Calvinball works so well on the page precisely *because* it is impossible to play — at least at Calvin's level. Watterson is savvy enough to only show us a couple of moments in a given Calvinball game: when every element is caught in an exhilarating state of flux, when all of its momentum could spin off thrillingly in a new direction at a moment's notice, and when ordering a transgressing player to sing something called "The Very Sorry Song," complete with over-the-top backup vocals, feels like the best idea you and your friends will ever have. As an idea, Calvinball feels like a work of harebrained genius. But unfrozen from time, it's a mess. It isn't a coincidence that while many popular fictional games have crossed over and become real sports, Calvinball has only ever spawned a couple of half-baked proposals on online message boards, each of which quickly fizzled out. Even Quidditch, a game originally conceived to be played by spell-casting wizards *in mid-air*, has had better luck as a competitive sport, now boasting its own World Cup and teams in dozens of countries around the world. Despite a nearly nonexistent barrier to entry — it could easily be played by any kid, at any time — this will never happen with Calvinball. That's because it's not so much a sport as it is the platonic ideal of a sport. Calvinball is an idea that is too fun in the abstract to survive being translated to the messy physical world. And even if it did catch on, what would happen once this anti-sport was infiltrated and, finally, taken over by the same kinds of jocks from the baseball storyline? The mind reels. No, Calvinball is forever insulated, and its purity forever protected, by its sheer impossibility — like an Escher staircase that can never be built, and thus can never be tarnished by a stranger's muddy footprints.

It's what Calvin would've wanted.

It was clear from very early on that *Calvin and Hobbes* was a hit. The only question was how high its ceiling could be. From its debut in 35 newspapers, the strip's popularity snowballed almost immediately, jumping to 250 newspapers in 1987 and to more than 600 in 1989. But it wasn't until the first year's worth of strips was published in book form that *Calvin and Hobbes* really became a phenomenon. Watterson's publisher, Andrews and McMeel, printed 50,000 copies for the debut collection's first run, and it would go through a total of 12 printings in the next 18 months alone. A second collection, *Something Under the Bed Is Drooling*, stayed on bestseller lists for an entire year. By this point, the strip was being translated into multiple languages and appearing in nearly 900 newspapers each morning.

The introduction to that initial, self-titled book collection was written by *Doonesbury* creator Garry Trudeau, who was one of the first to put the strip's unique sense of imagination and use of layered, conflicting realities into words. "Anyone who's done time with a small child knows that reality can be highly situational," Trudeau wrote. "The utterance which an adult knows to be a 'lie' may well reflect a child's deepest conviction, at least the moment it pops out. Fantasy is so accessible, and it is joined with such force and frequency, that resentful parents like Calvin's assume they are being manipulated, when the truth is far more frightening: they don't even exist. The child is both king and keeper of this realm, and he can be very choosy about the company he keeps."[21]

But despite the runaway success of his strip, all was not well for Watterson. Privately, he struggled with the daily demands of the job, not to mention the increasing pressure from his syndicate to license the strip's characters for merchandising.

By the spring of 1991, after much thought, Watterson decided to take a break. For readers of the strip, however, there was no warning. On May 4, a new *Calvin and Hobbes* appeared in the morning paper, just as it had every day for the past five years. Calvin, careening through the forest on his wagon, tells Hobbes he doesn't like the concept of being in the right place at the right time. So he decides he's going to just hang out in the right place indefinitely — "and if the right place is in front of the drug store, we could read comic books while we wait!" But the following day, there was no new *Calvin and Hobbes* strip in its place. Nor the next morning, nor the one after that.

For the next nine months, Bill Watterson disappeared, taking Calvin and his pet tiger with him.

3

Tough Sledding

On its most basic level, a comic strip is about the relationship between the artist and their piece of paper. It's only later that more people get involved: readers, editors, and, at the highest level, syndicates. And that's where things get messy.

Watterson's relationship with his syndicate was always uneasy. Certainly, he was grateful to Universal for green-lighting the strip in the first place. For any cartoonist trying to crack the mainstream funny pages, syndicates were pretty much the only game in town. And that meant the power structure was tilted accordingly. Watterson's repeated attempts to get a strip — any strip — through the door showed that he was at least willing to playing by the syndicate's rules. Unfortunately, that amenability also meant signing away the bulk of his power right off the bat. The contract Watterson initially signed for *Calvin and Hobbes* was standard, according to his editor, Lee Salem: the cartoonist would split all revenue with the syndicate 50-50, including the fees for each paper the strip appeared in and the royalties earned from any book collections. Watterson was also poised to earn half of any merchandising royalties the strip might earn, but it was Universal that would have final say on which products got made.

For most cartoonists, this arrangement isn't a problem. After all, licensing can be an extremely lucrative source of secondary income — if not the end goal of doing the strip, then at least a happy side effect. But Watterson took an unusually hard-line approach, especially for a young, unproven cartoonist at the beginning of his career. When the licensing offers started to roll in, Watterson reflexively turned them down. All of them. This left a rapidly growing pile of money on the table, half of which wasn't even his. It was only a matter of time until his syndicate decided to step in and enforce the fine print.

Watterson's commitment to his ideals wasn't forged on the spot, however. In fact, it can be traced back to his very first dealings with syndicates in general. In early 1984, just before Universal's rival United passed on *Calvin and Hobbes*, they flew Watterson all the way out to New York City to make him what must have sounded like a very unusual proposition. Higher-ups at the syndicate still weren't sold on Watterson's strip as it then stood, but United's marketing department had recently acquired the rights to a character called Robotman, who they felt had huge potential as a merchandising and animation property. He just needed a comic strip to call home. The question, then: was Watterson willing to incorporate Robotman into *Calvin and Hobbes* as a major, recurring character? If so, then United would reconsider the strip, and its odds of being accepted would jump that much higher.

This was a major test for the budding cartoonist. On the one hand, here was a clear path toward not just publication, but a lot of money from the inevitable licensing, too. As Watterson told *Honk* magazine, "They had envisioned a character as a product — toy lines, television show, everything — and they wanted a strip written around the character."[22] The syndicate didn't even seem to much care *how* Robotman was worked into the strip. He just had to be there.

And on the other hand, there was Watterson's gut feeling that this was a really bad idea.

For many of his peers, such a dilemma would have been easy to reconcile. How hard would it have been, really, to whip up a storyline where one of Calvin's homemade inventions goes haywire and takes on a life of its own? Besides, the line between compromise and selling out has always been blurry. You can't get published without making some sacrifices. Heck, the robot might even open up new possibilities for future stories.

But Watterson drew a line in the sand and said no. "It really went against my idea of what a comic strip should be," he said.[23] Even when the alternative — and not a far-fetched one, at that point — was not being published at all, Watterson decided he wasn't willing to start his career with such a drastic artistic concession. He knew if he opened a door like that on day one, he would have no way of closing it again later on. Accepting a foreign character into the strip would also mean letting other people, however indirectly, into his artistic process. "It's cartooning by committee," Watterson said, "and I have a moral problem with that. It's not art then."[24] Privately, the United editor who was told to organize the meeting, Sarah Gillespie, agreed with him, and their meeting in New York quickly stalled. "My impression was that [the proposal] was never really considered," she said later.[25] (United was, however, eventually able to convince another young cartoonist, Jim Meddick, to take on the Robotman project; the ensuing strip also debuted in 1985, and while the promised merchandising landslide never really happened, the strip lives on today as *Monty*, reimagined around a geeky inventor.)

Part of the problem, Watterson said, was that his sensibility didn't lend itself to the strict confines of a merchandising line. "*Calvin and Hobbes* isn't a gag strip," he told *The Comics Journal* in 1989. "It has a punchline, but the strip is about more than that. The humor is situational, and often episodic. It relies on conversation, and the development of personalities and relationships. These aren't concerns you can wrap up neatly in a clever little saying . . . Note pads and coffee mugs just aren't appropriate vehicles for what I'm trying to do here."[26] Adapting the strip to merchandising, Watterson felt, would sap it of the appeal that made the merchandise a profitable idea in the first place.

His syndicate clearly disagreed. Or, at least, they felt that the strip's achievements would not be wholly annihilated by the existence of a stuffed Hobbes doll for sale in department stores. Again, the final decision was technically out of Watterson's hands, but Universal also wasn't keen to ruin its working relationship with one of its star creators over a couple of action figure proposals. So for years the two parties found themselves at an impasse: the syndicate trying to get Watterson to warm up to the possibilities of licensing, and Watterson flat-out refusing every time. For all of Universal's attempts to tread softly around the fact that they had the right to license the strip if they wanted to, Watterson didn't even bother trying to sound conciliatory. "The strip is about more than jokes," he told *The Comics Journal*.[27] "I think the syndicate would admit this if they would start looking at my strip instead of just the royalty checks. Unfortunately, they are in the cartoon business only because it makes money, so arguments about artistic intentions are never very persuasive to them."*

No, Watterson could not be bought, and he wanted people to know it. He did allow that some strips were better suited for licensing and adaptation than others, and that "other people's strips aren't my job."[28] But in the case of *Calvin and Hobbes*, at least, he felt there was something larger — and more permanent — at stake. "The world of a comic strip is much more fragile than people realize," he said. "Once you've given up its integrity, that's it. I want to make sure that never happens."[29]

---

* Or take this, from his 1989 speech "The Cheapening of the Comics": "Syndicates . . . use their position of power to extort rights they do not deserve." Or this, from his commencement speech at Kenyon College a year later: "It never occurred to me that a comic strip I created would be at the mercy of a bloodsucking corporate parasite called a syndicate." Ouch, man.

Perhaps in moments of weakness, Watterson did agree to the creation of a couple of products: a pair of 16-month wall calendars (for 1988–1989 and 1989–1990), a promotional t-shirt for the Smithsonian exhibit *Great American Comics: 100 Years of Cartoon Art* (reprinting the Sunday strip in which Calvin makes a series of faces for the camera), and a rare 1993 children's textbook called *Teaching with Calvin and Hobbes*, copies of which now routinely fetch thousands of dollars online. But these were subject to Watterson's whims, and were clearly not the blockbuster items Universal had in mind — nor what *Calvin and Hobbes* readers were clamoring for. As the strip took off, big-name potential collaborators like Jim Henson, George Lucas, and Steven Spielberg would all come knocking (Spielberg twice). Watterson didn't even return their phone calls.

The strip's runaway success was also affecting Watterson on a personal level. As someone who relished his privacy and solitude, the cartoonist was quickly overwhelmed by new demands on his time from fans and media alike. His readers sent him piles of mail, pushing for autographs and original drawings; others looked up his phone number and called his house directly. "They all want something," Watterson griped to his local paper when the *Plain Dealer* started carrying the strip in early 1986.[30] The media wanted him, too. Watterson did grant occasional interviews in those early years, but after the tone of a profile in the *Los Angeles Times* rubbed him the wrong way, he called Salem and told him that was it. No more interviews, period. "Besides disliking the diminishment of privacy and the inhibiting quality of feeling watched, I valued my anonymous, boring life," Watterson wrote in the introduction to *The Complete Calvin and Hobbes*. "In fact, I didn't see how I could write without it."[31] After moving around Ohio, in 1990 Watterson decamped to Santa Fe, New Mexico, where he and his wife, Melissa, tried to reclaim their anonymity by living under her maiden name and delisting their telephone number. He did no interviews, nor did he show up to accept any of the industry awards he kept winning.

Still, these pressures — compounded by the grind of putting out a daily comic strip, plus the now-annual book collections, many of which contained new drawings and stories — continued to wear away at Watterson. So, in 1991, he went to Universal and demanded a new contract. "I was an unknown cartoonist when I started, and my contractual disadvantage reflected my nonexistent bargaining power when I got the job," Watterson wrote in *The Complete Calvin and Hobbes*. "Five years later, I was a big enough gorilla that I could turn the tables."[32] Watterson now wanted it in writing that the syndicate would be unable to license *Calvin and Hobbes* without his permission (which he had no intention of granting); otherwise, he would walk away from the strip forever, at which point the syndicate could, at least technically, hire someone else to replace him. Nobody doubted Watterson's sincerity. And while it must have pained Universal to seal off a tap that had, by Salem's estimate, tens of millions of dollars' worth of potential revenue behind it ("We could've made a fortune that would have been split two ways — it would've been two fortunes," he told me[33]), the syndicate also knew it was the only way of moving forward with Watterson onside.

Eventually, anyway. Because the *other* result of the contract renegotiations had to do with time off, which, in the cartooning business, typically doesn't exist. If a creator wants time off, it's up to them to bank the requisite number of strips ahead of time. Watterson's new deal, however, included not one but two extended breaks from the strip, each nine months long and the first to begin in May of that year.

The new contract may have been inevitable, but it exacted a heavy toll on both parties nonetheless, in a process that Watterson described later as "personally traumatic."[34] In *The Complete Calvin and Hobbes*, he wrote that for years afterward, the fight for control of the strip "poisoned what had been a happy relationship with my syndicate, and in my disillusionment and disgust at being pushed to the wall, I lost the conviction that I wanted to spend my life cartooning."[35] For the rest of 1991, at least, Watterson stepped away from the drawing board, enjoying the Spiff-like landscapes of New Mexico and recharging his creative batteries. (He also spent three months stuck sitting on a grand jury.) Readers were understandably shocked and saddened by the strip's sudden absence from their morning routines. Watterson's only explanation came via a playful but cryptic press release distributed by his syndicate: "The strip requires a great deal of research," he wrote, "and I need to do more interplanetary exploration and paleontology work before I continue."[36]

Even if Watterson felt drained by the demands of the strip, there was little evidence of this on the page. On the contrary: by 1991, *Calvin and Hobbes* was consistently dunking on pretty much all of its competition, and kept finding ways to push its own limits further and further. Watterson was confidently dropping ambitious, multi-week story arcs, introducing readers to the duplicator one month and deranged mutant killer monster snow goons the next. At the same time, he was testing out new drawing styles to accommodate Calvin's growing number of fantasy worlds, experimenting with new panel sizes and color palettes in the Sunday strips, and casually dropping references to Socrates, the Emancipation Proclamation, and *Doctor Zhivago*. "One of the jokes I really like," Watterson said later, in *Exploring Calvin and Hobbes*, "is that the fantasies are drawn more realistically than reality, since that says a lot about what's going on in Calvin's head."[37] The public, meanwhile, ate it all up. By the time of Watterson's first sabbatical, the strip was running in more than 1,800 newspapers, and the eight book collections published by that point had each sold more than a million copies in their first year. *Calvin and Hobbes* was that rare beast powered as much by critical acclaim as by commercial appeal, sweeping newspaper reader polls and industry awards alike. To pretty much any external onlooker, the strip was in the midst of a golden age the likes of which hadn't been seen in the comics pages for a long time.

There were clues, however, that Watterson wasn't happy — mainly the strips in which Calvin ventriloquized the exact problems his creator was having with his syndicate. "There were some very tough days in that period," Salem said later. "I regret to say that some of our discussions impacted his creative process and you can see those dark strains in the strip."[38] To Watterson's credit, most of the in-strip infighting made a certain amount of sense when put in Calvin's mouth, as he spent enough time railing against the unfairness of life anyway. Plus, Watterson was self-aware enough to put himself on the losing end of the argument more often than not.

These strips were sprinkled throughout the late '80s and early '90s, but they're spotted easily enough. Basically, just watch for those times Calvin takes a loud, angry, rhetorically torqued stance in fights that are obviously unwinnable, like needing to take a bath. "I stand *firm* in my belief of what's right!" he yells in one such strip, one arm raised defiantly. "I *refuse* to compromise my principles." Two panels later, he's in the tub. "I don't *need* to compromise my principles," Calvin says, his face now blank, "because they don't have the slightest bearing on what happens to me anyway." Later, in the *Tenth Anniversary Book*, Watterson readily admitted the subtext behind these strips. "Cartoons such as these helped me laugh at my predicament at a time when very little about it seemed funny," he wrote.[39]

Most of Watterson's protests, however, were delivered via the Sunday strips. There, with the added tool of color at his disposal, Watterson came up with more elaborate ways of dramatizing the arguments he was having behind the scenes. In one, Watterson draws nearly the whole thing in a dramatic monochrome, only to reveal in the final panel that Calvin is arguing with his dad (everyone now back in full color) about the six-year-old's tendency to see everything in terms of black and white. "Sometimes that's the way things are!!" Calvin yells back, arms outstretched above his head, echoing his creator's sentiments exactly. ("Best of all," Watterson later added, "I only needed to color one panel."[40]) More than one Sunday strip from this period saw Watterson experimenting with a fractured or neo-cubist drawing style — admittedly kind of a long way to go for a joke about seeing multiple perspectives, but the inventiveness of the drawings always carried the day. Calvin had a refreshing refusal to accept the lesson, too: "You're still wrong, Dad."

It was no coincidence that this more expansive format was Watterson's preferred venue for protest, because the Sunday strips otherwise drove him nuts. Weekday strips could already be shrunk or squished to fit whatever space a given newspaper had available, but Sundays were taken even further out of the cartoonist's hands. Here, convention dictated that each strip include three rows of panels, organized in such a way that a newspaper could either use the strip as it was submitted, reorder the panels so that they fit into a shorter, wider space, or else *remove the top row of panels entirely*, without so much as asking permission first. This created a byzantine story structure where cartoonists couldn't even guarantee that readers would see the full story they drew — it's also why most Sunday *Calvin and Hobbes* strips from the early years included seemingly unrelated gags in the first two panels. Watterson did this intentionally, so that these panels could be safely discarded without affecting the main thrust of the strip that followed, and he resented the wasted real estate every time.

This arrangement would be frustrating for any cartoonist. But Watterson was in a position to do something about it, which led to his final demand from the contract renegotiations: no more chopping. Beginning in 1992, when Watterson returned from sabbatical, all *Calvin and Hobbes* Sundays would be sold as full half-page blocks only. This would allow Watterson to draw the strip in any format he liked, with any number of panels, and, critically, without those throwaway panels at the top. If editors didn't like this arrangement, well, they were under no obligation to buy the Sunday strips. Still, the demand was unprecedented, and it sent a shockwave through the comics community. Universal told Watterson to prepare for a mass exodus; but while there was no shortage of outrage from newspaper editors, in the end, very few actually cancelled. Why? As one editor put it, "We had two choices. We could either keep *Calvin*, or take out more fire insurance."[41] The strip was just that beloved. Like Watterson's sabbatical — during which newspapers were essentially paying for nine months of re-runs — the Sunday renegotiations were a small but potentially significant victory for creators' rights. They forced editors to swallow their pride and accept that, in this case at least, the scales of power were starting to shift back in the cartoonist's favor.

We've already seen the ways Calvin used fantasy to create fully formed alternate realities and thereby escape the drudgery of his everyday life. But he was equally likely to use his imagination as a means of grappling with and making sense of the world. And as with Watterson's real-world conflicts, these encounters tended to come on Calvin's own terms, and in single-minded pursuit of his own goals. Watterson was able to succeed, ultimately, thanks to his dedicated readership and clout in the cartooning world — but things are harder when you're a socially ill-adjusted six-year-old.

One of the strip's earliest recurring bits is Calvin treating his dad like a politician, agitating for things like later bedtimes by reframing his complaints as polling numbers and threatening Dad with the prospect of having to run for re-election. This is at first glance a kid's cute impression of adulthood, Calvin's version of dressing up in his dad's clothes. But these strips, which were the favorites of Watterson's idol Charles Schulz, also reveal something critical about the boy's personality. Calvin tries to use this larger political framework — something he has no real understanding of, and which he has clearly absorbed piecemeal via the television — to make sense of the much smaller territory that is his everyday life. Politics is thus a kind of fantasy in its own right, projected by Calvin onto his reality in an attempt to improve it.

At the same time, the Dad-as-politician gags opened a window for the parent to connect with his permanently spaced-out kid. Whenever Dad tries to sit down and have a real conversation with his son — often around the dreaded concept of "building character" — Calvin shuts down. He tunes out. Within seconds, he's a galaxy away, in full Spaceman Spiff mode. It's only through the veneer of fantasy, with Calvin imagining himself as a professional pollster (complete with hand-drawn charts), that the two of them have anything approaching actual dialogue. Of course, Calvin's dad spends the majority of these strips amused but contrarian, turning the rubric of politics back toward his son:

CALVIN: If you're thinking of running for "Dad" again, you'd better get your campaign in gear. Frankly, the polls look grim. I don't think you've got much of a shot at keeping the office.

DAD: I take comfort in the fact that not many people would want it.

CALVIN: Flippant remarks have a way of haunting candidates, you know.

Like all kids, Calvin's attention is most easily held through games and imaginative play. But in his case, there are no other options. If you want any hope of him actually learning something, your only bet is to come at it sideways, sneaking bits of nutritional wisdom inside a thick candy coating.

As it happens, Calvin's parents serve as the strip's primary tether to the real world, providing swift, often humorless reminders to their son that the physics of Spaceman Spiff, or the politics of Dad's re-election campaign, do not apply beyond the confines of his own head. Young readers of the strip likely took this reading at face value — every hero needs obstacles to rail against — and moved on. Yet Calvin's parents also gave the strip's older readers a more age-appropriate counterpoint to the pint-sized chaos agent at the comic's core. That adult perspective most often manifested itself as an all-purpose wet blanket that doused Calvin's antics before they could even get started, which is in line with the tendency for grown-up readers to discount Hobbes's agency out of hand just because it "defies physics" and "isn't possible." (Killjoys.) In general, the strip wasn't afraid to use the same two-tiered joke system that you see in every Pixar movie today, where certain bits are expressly designed to fly over younger readers' heads but straight at the adults in the room (see: Dad's repeated refrain that instead of having Calvin, they could've adopted a dachshund).

But that's not to say the parents' imaginations have withered entirely. Just as Calvin's dad sometimes goes along with the political shtick, there are moments when his mom gets creative in the kitchen — not in terms of the food itself, but in how it's marketed to her six-year-old critic. In one Sunday strip, Calvin gives Mom his usual plugged-nose routine about how disgusting dinner smells. But when she casually rebrands the stuffed peppers on the stove as monkey heads, his eyes light up, and the tone of the entire meal improves. In moments like these, older readers see their loyalties suddenly challenged: rather than living vicariously through Calvin alone, they see their actual on-page proxies learn to let fantasy back into their lives, too. And if fantasy isn't only for kids, then maybe — just maybe — older readers might be willing to re-embrace their own imaginations the same way Calvin's parents have, however briefly.

In addition to politics, another world whose jargon Calvin seems to have absorbed, seemingly by accident, is that of modern art. From the beginning, Watterson saw Calvin as a flexible character: in one strip, smarter than all the adults, and in the next, the most clueless kid in the class — in other words, an awful lot like an actual six-year-old. "Calvin was never just one thing," Watterson said in *Exploring Calvin and Hobbes*. "He could function in a number of different ways. If I was thinking about some issue in current affairs, I could use Calvin to talk about it. If I just wanted to do something silly, I could use Calvin for *that*."[42] So it shouldn't come as a surprise, really, that whenever Calvin took to the wintery outdoors and started playing around with snowmen, he suddenly gained the lofty vocabulary of a gallery-goer with a full glass of wine.

The first time Calvin indulged his inner artist was in 1989, when he built little snow effigies representing everyone he hated, with sadistic plans to watch them slowly melt. (Hobbes: "I wasn't aware you even knew this many people.") But the snowman motif really took off in the strip's second half, postsabbatical. In one of Watterson's very first free-form Sunday strips, from February 16, 1992, Calvin bemoans the lack of craftsmanship in the modern world — a point he underscores by meticulously crafting a snowball, then signing it, before taking aim at Susie. A few days later, Calvin has turned his eye to snowmen, debating with Hobbes over what's more *avant garde*: intentionally ugly creatures with names like "Bourgeois Buffoon," or traditional-looking snowmen that tap into a '50s-throwback movement Calvin dubs "neo-regionalism." Watterson had already drawn plenty of strips of Calvin in the wintertime, of course. But once this premise, with its quintessential blend of youthful play and knotted jargon, had been articulated, it became one of his go-to devices for the remainder of the strip's run. "I enjoy studying art," Watterson wrote in the *Tenth Anniversary Book*, "but the field certainly attracts its share of pretentious blowhards."[43]

Of course, Calvin's talents in the medium of snow went far beyond those of a typical six-year-old. He could make giant snow snakes, prisoners with cannonball holes through their torsos, house-eating lizards whose outlines were only visible from the sky, giants peeking over the horizon, an all-snow version of Easter Island, and even — depending on whose version of reality you subscribe to — a fleet of murderous, multi-limbed snow goons. (Calvin, it should be said, protested his innocence in the latter case.) And when he wasn't doing the creating, Calvin was happy to take on the mantle of the beleaguered snow critic instead. In one Sunday strip, he walks down the sidewalk with Hobbes, offering his spontaneous review of the other would-be artists on his block. He scoffs at the cheap shock value of an anatomically correct female snowman, and even a single, abandoned ball of snow doesn't escape his withering appraisal: "Look, pal, there's no point expressing ideas if you can't make them understood! You're just babbling to yourself!"

Sometimes Calvin is cynical about the future of art in the face of commerce, as when he announces to Hobbes one Sunday that "style is exhausted and content is pointless," which is why he has signed his name on the snowy landscape itself and is now selling it for a cool million dollars. Hobbes demurs, saying it doesn't match his furniture. (Calvin then turns to the reader to deliver his response: "The problem with being *avant garde* is knowing who's putting on who.")

Other times, however, Calvin seems only too eager to embrace the decline of high culture. The very next day after signing the landscape, Calvin builds a frowning snowman, who is, he says, aware that he's doomed to melt and die. Hobbes asks if his life is meaningless. "Nope," says Calvin, rolling another snowball. "He's about to buy a big-screen TV."

Television occupies another interesting symbolic place in the strip's world. TV would seem to be exactly the kind of mental sedative that Calvin, a kid with an imagination that's always on the verge of boiling over, would run screaming from. Yet he is far from immune to its charms, even while admitting it's not a perfect user experience. "These television programs sure are rotten," he says to Hobbes in one early strip. "There isn't an ounce of imagination in the whole bunch. What bilge." But what's he going to do, *not* watch it? In the absence of more personalized options like Netflix or YouTube, Calvin has no choice but to point his eyeballs at whatever screen is available.

What TV offers him, aside from a chance to turn his brain off and see how little energy he can expend ("Notice how I keep my jaw slack, so my mouth hangs open"), is a window into the highly sought-after world of adults — one that extends beyond his parents' obsession with following rules and building character. Television, by contrast, is exciting and exotic. It tempts him with fantasies he's only dreamed of, as embodied by the alternately sexy and gory late-night movies he tries to watch on the sly, with irresistible names like *Cannibal Stewardess Vixens Unchained* and *Sorority Row Horror*. Television teaches him about adult pursuits like politics and art, which he then promptly tries to apply, half-remembered, to his own life. To Calvin, it even outstrips his own daily reality, as when he hurries through a sled ride outside because "there's a TV show on sledding I want to watch."

Again, in many ways, Calvin is the poster boy for the children of the late '80s and early '90s, unwittingly raised by countless hours of sitcoms and breaking-news soundbites. "This article says that by age six, most children have watched 5,000 hours of TV — a quarter of their waking lives!" Calvin says in one strip, horrified at how much he's missed out on. "I've been deprived of cultural references! I'm ignorant of amazing products!" But despite the general hysteria surrounding kids' TV habits at the time, Watterson remains ambivalent about the actual effect it has on his protagonist. For one thing, Calvin seems to be constitutionally incapable of becoming a truly passive media consumer. He's constantly soaking in material only to then adapt it for his own purposes, whether in conversation with his parents, games with Hobbes, or weaseling his way through a class project he hasn't prepared for. Plus, Watterson is quick to point out that TV didn't always have the moral high ground on other, supposedly more virtuous media. In a move that probably didn't endear Watterson any further to his editors, Calvin claims to love newspapers because "they give me what I want: antics, emotional confrontation, sound bites, scandal, sob stories, and popularity polls all packaged as a soap opera and horse race!" Or consider the Sunday strip where Calvin becomes hypnotized at the ultra-realistic, (literally) spine-shattering fight scenes in one of his comic books. When he takes a break to go watch a show, his mom scolds him: "There's too much violence on TV. Why don't you go read something?"

At times, Calvin's relationship with TV appears to be yet another of his fantasy worlds, where he assumes the part of the brain-dead viewer (perhaps the imagined six-year-old who's consumed north of 5,000 hours of the stuff) while also using what he watches as yet more fuel for his various imaginative escapades. This would explain the strip where he approaches the TV late one night and offers up the following prayer: "Oh greatest of the mass media, thank you for elevating emotion, reducing thought, and stifling imagination. Thank you for the artificiality of quick solutions and for the insidious manipulation of human desires for commercial purposes. This bowl of lukewarm tapioca represents my brain. I offer it in humble sacrifice. Bestow thy flickering light forever." By himself, pajama-clad, in the middle of the night, Calvin articulates TV's destructive tendencies better than most of its grown-up critics could. There are many ways to describe his viewing habits, but "lazy" is not one of them.

Television also gives Calvin another crucial outlet: the ability to relate, however briefly, to another person. This may sound over the top, but reading through the 3,000+ strips in the *Calvin and Hobbes* oeuvre, it is striking how little genuine human contact Calvin actually has. All of the usual social avenues for kids are, for him, dead ends. Hobbes is about as loyal a best friend as one could hope for, of course, but when it comes to people — the kind who are visible to everyone else — it's pretty tough sledding. In interviews, Watterson has resisted the idea that the strip is about friendship, but I would suggest an alternative. *Calvin and Hobbes* is, on a fundamental level, a strip about loneliness: the ways we keep it at bay, insulate ourselves from it, and, occasionally, when our options run out, give in to it. Imagination is a coping mechanism, and an extremely effective one at that. But even the most creative kid on earth can only outrun the abyss for so long.

One of the great touches of *Calvin and Hobbes* is that while Calvin has zero compatibility with most of the humans in his life, there are, in fact, several kindred spirits out there — but Calvin is so absorbed in his own world that's he unable to recognize them. And he doesn't even have to look that far; the first lives down the street. Despite her many appearances as Calvin's more intelligent foil, over the course of the strip we also get glimpses into the world as Susie Derkins sees it. In one such story, Susie asks Calvin if he wants to play, but he rejects her. Susie walks off, frustrated. "That stupid Calvin," she says. "He's so mean. All I try to do is be friends, and he treats me like I'm nobody. Well, who needs jerks like him anyway? I don't need him for a friend. I can have fun by myself!" The final panel pulls back to show Susie sitting on a rock in the woods, by herself, poking a stick into ground. A year later, she's in the same situation, crying over Calvin casually insulting her and imagining she has a hundred other friends. "*Then* I wouldn't care," she says to herself. "I'd say, 'Who needs *you*, Calvin? I've got a hundred other friends!'" But it isn't true, and Susie knows it. ". . . And as long as I'm dreaming," she adds at the end, "I'd like a pony." Susie is not an unimaginative kid, by any means. Elsewhere, we see her hosting elaborate tea parties with her own stuffed animals — she even ropes Calvin, temporarily, into more realistic, domestic games that Watterson draws in a goofy *Rex Morgan*–like homage. But with the kid who lives down the street being alternately cruel and aloof, without any siblings to play with (like Calvin, Susie is an only child), and, critically, without a magical stuffed animal to sub in for a best friend, Susie is left to feel her loneliness that much more acutely.

Adults that Calvin can relate to are also in short supply, in large part because most of the grown-ups he interacts with are figures of authority, which immediately get his back up. But there is one adult who Calvin seems to get along with quite well: Uncle Max. This character, the looser, mustachioed brother of Calvin's dad, only appeared in one story arc, early in the strip's run, and Watterson came to regret it. "After the story ran, I realized that I hadn't established much identity for Max, and that he didn't bring out anything new in Calvin," Watterson wrote in the *Tenth Anniversary Book*. He also posed a logistical problem, since he couldn't address either of Calvin's parents by name. "Max," Watterson concluded, "is gone."[44]

While it's true that the strip seemed cluttered when Max was there — three adults tended to dominate the frame, especially compared to the diminutive Calvin — it's also true that Max represented a possibility that no other adult in the subsequent strips would. Despite Calvin's worries about having a second uptight dad in the house, Max endears himself to Calvin right away. After picking Max up from the airport, Calvin introduces him to Hobbes, and his uncle takes Calvin's descriptions at their word. When Calvin describes Hobbes's "mandibles of death," Max agrees, and straight-facedly retreats to the kitchen. Once he's out of the room, Calvin and Hobbes are nearly giddy. "Ol' Uncle Max seems pretty sharp," Calvin says. "Hard to believe he's related to Dad." At dinner that night, Calvin asks to sit next to Max — a rare sign of affection that is only partly undermined by Calvin planting a whoopee cushion on his seat.

One reason Watterson may have felt Max didn't add anything to the strip is because, at times, he reads like a grown-up version of Calvin. At one point, Max expresses concern to Calvin's mom that Calvin spends all his time playing with Hobbes. "Do you worry about that?" he asks her. "Shouldn't he be playing with real friends?" To her credit, Calvin's mom defends him, asking whether Max didn't have an imaginary friend when he was a kid. Leaning against the counter, Max replies, "Sometimes I think *all* my friends have been imaginary." So by his own admission, Max isn't someone who doesn't understand Calvin's relationship with Hobbes; on the contrary, he sounds like someone who understands it all too well, and maybe even someone who's trying to help his nephew avoid future problems that he himself once faced. Calvin grows fonder of Max as his visit wears on, and even tries to board the plane with him at the last minute. It's not an overly serious storyline, all told. The jokes are still there. But this early relationship between Calvin and a sympathetic adult with a functioning imagination never gets repeated. For all the strip's experimentation with cardboard boxes, this, to me, is the story that comes closest to actual time travel.

There is one other person with whom Calvin finds an honest rapport. It comes in the strip's final months, on the heels of a solid decade's worth of rivalry that goes well beyond anything in Calvin's hormonal love-hate relationship with Susie. In the annals of *Calvin and Hobbes*, there may not be a character more diametrically opposed to Calvin and his worldview than his no-nonsense babysitter, Rosalyn — and their surprising, late-breaking reconciliation provided one final surprise in a strip full of them.

Rosalyn was the last of the strip's recurring characters to be introduced, debuting in a three-part story in May 1986, seven months after *Calvin and Hobbes* began. She was intended to be a throwaway character, but Watterson was surprised at how well she was able to intimidate the usually fearless Calvin, so he kept bringing her back. "Rosalyn's relationship with Calvin is pretty one-dimensional," Watterson allowed, "so babysitter stories got harder and harder to write, but for a later addition to the strip, she's worked pretty well."[45] Typically, Rosalyn was the straight woman to Calvin's antics, an easily irritated teen-ager who wielded her power like a tyrant, sending him to bed at a moment's notice whether the sun had set or not. Even the rigidness of Miss Wormwood's classroom still had enough give for Calvin to privately indulge in his Spaceman Spiff fantasies; being trapped in the house by himself with Rosalyn, on the other hand, who had zero tolerance for silliness — or fun in general — was his actual worst nightmare. This, in turn, nudged Calvin toward worse and worse behavior. It was a nice dynamic.

For the first half of the strip's run, Rosalyn would show up every year or so, strike fear into Calvin's heart, and then head home (but not before milking his parents for an advance on her next visit). Sometimes Calvin would temporarily gain the upper hand, like the time he pretended to flush her homework down the toilet, or when he locked her out of the house so he and Hobbes could eat an entire bag of Oreos. But Rosalyn usually held her own — and even when she didn't, it was only a matter of time until the cavalry came back home from their date and *really* let Calvin have it. After defeating Stupendous Man in a 15-part story in early 1990, however, Rosalyn wouldn't show up again on the page for more than five years, until the strip was winding down for good. It was to be her final appearance, and Watterson made sure it was a memorable one.

The story starts in familiar territory, with Calvin freaking out upon her arrival, and Rosalyn standing there with her arms crossed, frowning. But this time, she offers him a deal: if he doesn't give her any grief, they will stay up half an hour later than usual and play a game — of Calvin's choosing. And that can only mean one thing. "Get out the time-fracture wickets!" Calvin calls to Hobbes. "We're gonna play Calvinball!"

Rosalyn, of course, has never heard of the game. And at first, during an elaborate improvised song and then a segment where everyone has to talk in slow motion, she wishes she'd never given Calvin such an open-ended choice. "Thiisss gaaaame maaakes noooo sennnse!" she says. "It'sss aasss iffff you'rrrre maaakinnnggg iiiiit uuup aaas youuu gooo." Calvin turns to Hobbes, horrified: "She stumbled into the Perimeter of Wisdom! Run!!" Just like that, the game tilts in Rosalyn's favor as the babysitter figures out she can use the game's essential creativity against its creator. First, she decrees that Calvin has to catch a water balloon that she throws into the air. Then, while Calvin's busy doing that, she takes Hobbes prisoner. And finally, as Calvin prepares to soak them both, Rosalyn tags him with the babysitter flag. "What's the babysitter flag?" Calvin asks. "It means you must obey the babysitter," Rosalyn replies. And that means bedtime, at last.

Any time Watterson wrote a crossover strip was cause for celebration. There was the time Calvin's snowmen creations merged with a fantasy about dinosaurs, or the time Spaceman Spiff showed up during a family camping trip, or the time his cardboard box was hastily repurposed as a makeshift meeting room for the Get Rid Of Slimy girlS club (G.R.O.S.S.). And Rosalyn herself had already taken on Stupendous Man in her penultimate appearance. But given how close *Calvin and*

Hobbes was to ending its run, this story feels especially like a culmination: after years of take-no-prisoners fighting, Calvin finally makes peace with his greatest nemesis, and on his own terms, using one of his own private games as the medium. Remember, despite the reader's familiarity with Calvin's inner life, nobody else in the strip knows what really goes on in there. Not a single other person knows who Spaceman Spiff is, because Calvin never tells them. By and large, his imagination is just that — imaginary. Invisible to everyone else in his life. None of Calvin's parents, classmates, or teachers ever take the time to understand how his fantasy worlds operate, and he can't be bothered to explain them. Only Hobbes understands Calvin on this level. By teaching Rosalyn how to play Calvinball, Calvin is letting another person into his world in a way that he never has before. It's an extremely vulnerable place for him. And, to Rosalyn's credit, she doesn't laugh in his face, or sneer at his childish delusions. She takes him seriously. Not only that: she *joins in*. Like Uncle Max before her, Rosalyn offers Calvin a moment of true imaginative connection — and with it, a glimmer of hope that his future might actually have room for other people after all.

The end of *Calvin and Hobbes* came faster than almost anyone at the time expected. Watterson had told his syndicate as early as the contract renegotiations in 1990–1991 that he was considering ending the strip within a year or so. That struck fear into the heart of Universal, who — having already forgone millions of dollars in licensing money — were banking on a steady stream of book sales and newspaper revenue for many years to come. Watterson was, after all, one of the syndicate's star cartoonists, and *Calvin and Hobbes* was a critical and commercial juggernaut. Hence the sabbaticals. Despite perceptions at the time about the "uppity" cartoonist,[46] these were actually Universal's idea, not Watterson's, as a means of prolonging the strip's total run. Salem says the two nine-month breaks were designed to do two things: "Give [Watterson] a little time off, so he could catch his breath, but also help stretch out the contract a bit."[47] The goal was to extend the run to an even ten years — which would carry the strip to the end of 1995.

By the time Watterson returned from his second sabbatical, on January 1, 1995, there were signs that his creative flame was starting to flicker. The daily strips had started to lean more and more on simple jokes and observations. The drawings were sparer. And there was less dialogue, and longer silences. At the same time, Watterson's Sunday strips were becoming more elaborate than ever. It's hard to find one from that entire last year with a traditional visual structure; more often you'd find intricate rhyming poems, 32-part flipbook animations, or first-person POV sled rides off cliffs, complete with all-black panels whenever Hobbes has closed his eyes. "My self-imposed rule was that the Sunday strip had to be something that would work no other way," Watterson said later. "So that generally pushed the Sundays toward elaborate drawings or ideas that required many panels."[48] Some of these strips, though technically stunning, have the feel of an artist more interested in the stray details than in the story he's telling, as if Watterson were doodling around the margins of a school assignment — which is how Raumfahrer Rolf was first born, all those years earlier. After relentlessly pushing the envelope for so many strips, challenging his readers to expand their conceptions of what a daily comic strip could do, this was the first time Watterson's own imagination appeared to be coming back to earth.

Then the other shoe dropped. On November 9, the following letter ran alongside the strip in hundreds of papers across North America:

> I will be stopping *Calvin and Hobbes* at the end of the year. This was not a recent or an easy decision, and I leave with some sadness. My interests have shifted, however, and I believe I've done what I can do within the constraints of daily deadlines and small panels. I am eager to work at a more thoughtful pace, with fewer artistic compromises. I have not yet decided on future projects, but my relationship with Universal Press Syndicate will continue.
>
> That so many newspapers would carry *Calvin and Hobbes* is an honor I'll long be proud of, and I've greatly appreciated your support and indulgence over the last decade. Drawing this comic strip has been a privilege and a pleasure, and I thank you for giving me the opportunity.
>
> Sincerely,
> Bill Watterson[49]

For readers, this was another shock, and for some, a betrayal. Hadn't they just endured two long, agonizing sabbaticals, which were supposed to get Watterson back into fighting form? In the comfortingly familiar world of daily comics, where creators almost never took time off, Watterson had already been absent for 18 months over the past five years. Plus, was this really the end of the strip? Watterson's letter still stands out for its strangely stiff yet dismissive tone — the creator of one of the most beloved comic strips of the 20th century leaves, seemingly on a dime, "with some sadness"? *Some*? Well, as long as his relationship with his syndicate is continuing . . .

Of course, the decision to step away was always Watterson's to make. And it wasn't his job to assuage the feelings of his readers, either. But the abruptness of this farewell letter, as well as how untroubled by his decision Watterson sounded in it, was a blow that many readers were slow to recover from.

As Watterson prepared to retreat from public life even further, his protagonist, too, was always ultimately happiest when away from other people. Calvin was primarily a kid of action, but he did have an introspective side. Whenever Watterson wanted to showcase both at once, he sent Calvin and Hobbes out on a wagon ride (or, in the winter, onto Calvin's sled). These strips were a mainstay from the beginning, and they allowed Calvin to chew on life's big issues while simultaneously trying to avoid the dizzying hills, forests, and cliffs that seemed to surround his house. The joke was a natural by-product of the disconnect between Calvin's highfalutin philosophizing and the rickety red wagon he sat on, narrowly avoiding sudden death, with his fuzzy best friend riding shotgun. "Calvin's woods [are] important to the strip," Watterson wrote in the *Tenth Anniversary Book*, "because it's the place where Calvin and Hobbes can get away from everyone and be themselves. The solitude of the woods brings out Calvin's small, but redeeming, contemplative side."[50]

So it was only fitting that for the final *Calvin and Hobbes* strip, Watterson sent Calvin out on one last existential careen through the great outdoors. Luckily, the December 31, 1995, strip fell on a Sunday, letting Watterson conclude his ten-year, 3,100-strip run using the boundless, more expansive palette that he'd become famous for. (A little infamous, too, depending on which newspaper editor you were talking to.) In the first panel, Calvin and Hobbes run through fresh, waist-deep snow into the woods. Calvin's in full winter gear. Hobbes is wearing a red scarf. They're in full color, but the rest of the snowy landscape around them is all white. The pair marvel at how the snowfall has changed the woods. "A new year . . . a fresh, clean start!" says Calvin. "It's like having a big white sheet of paper to draw on!" Hobbes adds. They lay the sled down on the ground and climb on. "It's a magical world, Hobbes, ol' buddy," Calvin says. "Let's go exploring!" And together they take off down the hill, wild grins on their faces, already fading into the blank, snowy distance by panel's end.

Once again, Calvin and Hobbes were gone — only this time, it was for good.

4

Leave Bill Watterson Alone

Want to contact Bill Watterson, creator of *Calvin and Hobbes*, one of your favorite comic strips of all time? He doesn't have a publicist, or a personal website, or any social media accounts, or a publicly accessible email address. So here's what you do.

First, go to the website for his book publisher, Andrews McMeel. Then click on the "Contact Us" page, and scroll down to the bottom. There, you'll see an entire section called "Contacting Bill Watterson." Success! Well, until you read the next part: "Unfortunately, Bill Watterson is not available for media interviews."[51] OK, sure. He was burned by the *L.A. Times* in the '80s and never really recovered from it. Fair enough. But what about regular, salt-of-the-earth fans? "If you are not with the media," the website continues, "but are hoping to receive an autographed copy of *The Complete Calvin and Hobbes*, or wish to have correspondence forwarded to Bill Watterson, we are sorry to report that at his request, we do not forward such correspondence his way for the sheer fact that he would be unable to keep up with the overwhelming demand."

The truth is, you aren't going to contact Watterson. I mean, you *could*, if you really wanted to — there are two million people in the Greater Cleveland area, where Watterson is said to currently live, and that number of doors is at least theoretically knockable. Or maybe you're a teenaged Romanian hacker who knows how to reverse-engineer the right phone number. But you aren't going to. This is as much a request as a statement of fact. Watterson doesn't want you to find him, which is reason enough to stay home. And given his public stance on the issue, odds are you aren't going to come away with a positive encounter even if you do manage to track him down.

And yet . . . you still kind of want to, don't you?

When a piece of art resonates, it's natural for fans to also feel a connection to the creator. And in the 21st century, that itch is more easily scratched than ever. Creators have figured out that they can use social media, as well as forums like the expanding (and seemingly never-ending) convention circuit, to connect with their fans directly. Fans, in turn, have gotten used to that ongoing access; in many ways, we've become spoiled by it. Access is what allowed fans to get direct updates from George R. R. Martin, through his blog, about the state of his unfinished A Song of Ice and Fire series (the basis for HBO's *Game of Thrones*) — and access is also what enabled those same fans to start making demands of him and how he spends his free time while working on a new book. "Some of you are angry that I watch football during the fall," Martin wrote in 2009. "After all, as some of you like to point out in your emails, I am 60 years old and fat, and you don't want me to 'pull a Robert Jordan' [referring to the author who died before completing his lengthy Wheel of Time series] on you and deny you your book."[52] The key phrase there: *your book*. Before the author has even written it. As Martin's example makes clear, the line between privilege and entitlement is thinning and can now easily be crossed without fans even realizing they've done it.

Bill Watterson will turn 60 in June 2018, the year this book is released. As of this writing, I have no reason to fear for his physical or mental health. In the one file photo that continues to circulate, at least, he looks slim and hale. His lack of interest in the internet suggests a healthy attitude toward screen time, which never hurts. The biggest difference between him and Martin, however, is that Watterson isn't holding the final pieces of a beloved work of art inside his head. Watterson has already given *Calvin and Hobbes* fans everything he could, and then one day he stopped — not because he went broke, or because the strip was canceled, or because his hands or brain stopped working. As Watterson put it in his farewell note to readers, his "interests" had "shifted." He was run-down, and maybe a little bored. He stopped because he was done.

Why was — and is — it so hard for Watterson's fans to accept this? "Still, people come up to me, and they grieve the loss of *Calvin and Hobbes*," Lucy Caswell, curator of the Billy Ireland Cartoon Library and Museum, said in 2010.[53] The strips were published in book form almost immediately, and today we have the entirety of the strip's run available in a lovingly assembled deluxe box set, authorized by its creator, to boot. We have rough drafts, assorted behind-the-scenes material, and even sketches of abandoned strip ideas. How can that not be enough? Maybe it was the readers' sheer love of the characters, and the understandable ache that came with knowing they'd never see them take off on another ill-advised adventure together. Maybe the lack of merchandising made the strip seem unusually ephemeral, with fewer connections to the world as it kept spinning post-1995. Or maybe it had something to do with the medium itself, since comic-strip creators so rarely leave the business of their own volition; as Watterson later wrote in *The Complete Calvin and Hobbes*, "The voluntary ending of successful comic strips is something new."[54]

I have another theory.

The reason *Calvin and Hobbes* still leaves readers with a sense of loss — the reason more than 400,000 Twitter users, and over a million Facebook users, subscribe to fan pages that post nothing but random old bootlegged images from the strip — isn't because Watterson walked away at the height of his powers. It's because of the *way* he did it. Watterson's departure was casual. Offhanded. He seemed totally untroubled by his decision. There was no teary press conference, no rambling, conflicted letter of appreciation for his readers and how much he'd miss them. There wasn't even the same note of pride (maybe smugness) that someone like Jerry Seinfeld gives off whenever he talks about taking his sitcom off the air when it was still number one in the ratings. To read Watterson's farewell note, and then to live for decades in a world where he never produced another comic strip, you'd think he felt . . . nothing.

To its fans, *Calvin and Hobbes* felt like a masterpiece. Yet Watterson's public statements suggested he saw it as nothing more than an interesting experiment, one that was easily discarded. No wonder readers felt betrayed. Imagine poring over a series of love letters only to later discover they'd been written in a rush, with the TV on in the background, while the person was on the phone with someone else. Not only were fans being denied further access to the strip they loved, but they were also being kept at a distance from the man who created it. Was it possible *C&H* fans were reading a level of love and thoughtfulness into the strip that simply wasn't reciprocated? Was their love of the strip a one-way relationship? And if Watterson's interests really had just shifted away from *Calvin and Hobbes* and into other avenues — well, what *were* those other avenues? Would fans ever get to see them? Or was Watterson just sitting on his couch, not doing much of anything, watching enough football to make George R. R. Martin blush?

In short, where has Watterson been since 1995? His fans have a right to know — don't they?

For decades now, Bill Watterson's name has carried an air of mystery and intrigue around it. *Calvin and Hobbes* being retired at the peak of its popularity was certainly a statement — but given Watterson's scant reasoning, fans found it difficult to take him at his word. In the absence of more detail, some of the creator's stronger opinions took on ever larger significance in readers' minds. The anti-merchandising stance. The belief that the comics page was going steadily downhill. And, of course, the lack of interest in becoming the celebrity that fans wanted him to be. Without an easily understood public persona, Watterson became a subject of almost endless fascination, an enigma whose motives were only partly understood and never fully believed.

Humans, as a rule, don't handle enigmas well. We demand answers and closure above all else. And so, over the years, some of the stauncher *C&H* fans — especially those who also happened to have media credentials — have chosen to interpret Watterson's withdrawal as a puzzle crying out to be solved.

In 1998, a reporter from the *Cleveland Plain Dealer* went out looking for Watterson and, to everyone's surprise, actually ended up talking to him at the front door of his home in Chagrin Falls, to which he'd recently returned. Watterson answered the door, wearing a paint apron over top of a white sweatshirt and jeans, but wouldn't allow the reporter, John C. Kuehner, to record or take any notes while they spoke informally. "He's very intelligent and wanted to discuss the merits of why he wasn't a public figure," Kuehner told the *Christian Science Observer* afterward. "He wanted to debate; it was almost collegiate."[55]

None of the others who followed Kuehner's example would be so lucky. Five years later, a reporter with the *Cleveland Scene* tried his luck, too, and came back with nothing but the mildly paranoid fantasy that every middle-aged stranger he passed was a potential Watterson in hiding. Gene Weingarten from the *Washington Post* gave it a shot of his own that same year, even offering a valuable first edition of one of Crockett Johnson's *Barnaby* books to Watterson's parents as a sweetener. Weingarten told them he would wait in a nearby hotel for as long as it took their son to decide to talk. The next day, he got a call, not from the cartoonist but from Lee Salem, Watterson's former editor, letting Weingarten down gently: it wasn't going to happen. He might as well just go home. So he did.

Nevin Martell's 2009 book *Looking for Calvin and Hobbes* includes the story of Weingarten's failed attempt in its prologue. But Weingarten's failure doesn't dissuade Martell, a music and food writer by trade, from trying again. "However," he admits, "it was depressing to know that the path ahead would be littered with the failures of reputable journalists who had given it their all, but to no avail."[56] Martell's book is the closest document we have to a biography of Watterson, and it contains a ton of fascinating new information about the cartoonist's life and early work. But that reporting is wrapped up inside a superfan's quest narrative that sees Martell devote nearly ten pages to his own thoughts about the letter he mails to Watterson's home, requesting an interview. (The eventual response, delivered again via Salem: "Why is he doing this? Who cares?"[57]) In the final chapters, Martell travels to Chagrin Falls, and through a lucky connection manages to convince Watterson's mother, Kathryn, to do an interview on the record. This was a journalistic coup of a sort, but it's pretty clear that Watterson wouldn't have been pleased once he found out about it. "This country has such an odd attachment to people in the limelight," his mother tells Martell, "and that's another reason that Bill does not want to be in the limelight. He doesn't appreciate that at all."[58]

The 2013 documentary *Dear Mr. Watterson* takes a similar approach, blending the autobiography of a superfan (in this case, the director Joel Allen Schroeder) with interviews with Watterson's peers and admirers in the cartooning world. Schroeder, too, wears his love of the strip on his sleeve, and he, too, makes the trek out to Chagrin Falls — as it happens, to meet up with Martell, who's in town to promote *Looking for Calvin and Hobbes*. The footage of Ohio's fall foliage is certainly evocative, but Schroeder's full-throated, even sycophantic, love of his subject fatally boxes his film in. The *New York Times* called the director "painfully earnest (and overly present)," and that about sums it up.[59]

By putting on the hats of journalists pursuing the public interest, rather than just a pair of nosy fans, Martell and Schroeder give themselves permission to get far closer to Watterson than they would otherwise dare. But if the goal of each is to unearth the Truth, why not go all in and head straight to the source? Martell tells us right away in his book that he has found Watterson's home address and phone number, after all. In the end, both he and Schroeder want to have it both ways: they want to publicly dispel the air of mystery surrounding Watterson, but they also want Watterson not to hate them for doing so. It doesn't really work like that in practice. You can either be a hard-nosed journalist, like the *Plain Dealer* reporter who put niceties to the side for the sake of his story, or you can respect your idol's wish for privacy. In trying to split the difference, the two most prominent pieces of commentary on *Calvin and Hobbes* to date leave both camps equally unsatisfied.

Even before *Calvin and Hobbes* left daily newspapers behind, Watterson started to garner a reputation as a recluse. He'd always felt he was able to express himself best through the strip, and he preferred to put his efforts there, rather than into the media or other public appearances. Nobody knew what he sounded, or even really looked, like; stories about the cartoonist were always accompanied by the same 1986 file photo, showing Watterson in a striped wool sweater, looking up from his drawing table and grinning like a mustachioed, bespectacled Cheshire Cat. Combine that scant audio-visual evidence with Watterson's testy relationship with his syndicate over merchandising, his pessimism about the state of the comics industry as a whole, and, especially, his lack of a follow-up project, and that reputation has snowballed to near-mythic proportions. When people write about Watterson these days, they tend to invoke names like J.D. Salinger and Thomas Pynchon. His whereabouts are only generally known. At long last, Watterson has insulated himself from the outside world.

Except, of course, that he hasn't, at all. For all of Watterson's reputation as a recluse — a label that, keep in mind, is never self-administered — he has popped up repeatedly in the public sphere since retiring from the strip. True, these appearances have often come without warning and according to Watterson's whims, and they seem to surprise even his collaborators. But with fame and fortune already established as nonstarters, Watterson appears to be freer than ever to quietly follow his inner muse wherever it takes him.

The first time anybody outside his inner circle heard from Watterson after the end of *Calvin and Hobbes* wasn't until a full four years later, when he re-emerged to wish one of his idols a fond farewell of his own. As Charles Schulz's *Peanuts* was due to wind down after nearly 50 years in print, Watterson wrote an ode to the strip for the *Los Angeles Times* on December 21, 1999. The piece reflects on some of Watterson's favorite elements of the strip, and in it he applauds Schulz for his "brilliant graphic shorthand and stylistic economy" and praises the strip as a singular achievement, even all these years later. "*Peanuts* is one of those magical strips that creates its own world," Watterson wrote. That world may be "a distortion of our own," but "we enter it on its terms, and, in doing so, see our world more clearly."[60]

Beyond being Watterson's first public commentary since ending his own strip, the article is noteworthy for a couple of reasons. First, Watterson shares the byline with his syndicate. This meant that he'd been true to his word, back in his farewell note, that he would continue working with Lee Salem and Universal — and was perhaps a hint that he still had a toe in the world of cartooning. But it also stands out because Watterson barely even gestures toward his own status as one of Schulz's peers in the cartooning world. In effect, Watterson is reverting to the kind of work he'd done before breaking into the field: as a critic, penning reviews and opinion pieces for his friend Rich West's magazine, *Target*. Rather than leaning on his own resumé and name recognition, Watterson chose to write a detailed appreciation of Schulz the craftsman, who invigorated daily comics with his emotional depth and the "quirky velocity and pressure" of his illustrations. For Watterson, the work, again, came above all else.

Eight years later, Watterson returned with another newspaper piece about *Peanuts*, this time a review of David Michaelis's 2007 biography *Schulz and Peanuts*, in the pages of the *Wall Street Journal*. It wasn't Watterson's idea; Mark Lasswell, then an editor in the paper's books department, was looking to assign a reviewer and wrote to Universal Press Syndicate as a kind of Hail Mary. To everyone's surprise, Watterson agreed. And if his earlier ode to *Peanuts* was a chance to exercise his dormant critical muscles, Watterson's *WSJ* review was a full-on flex. The piece reads like the work of a seasoned reviewer, with sharp, precise descriptions and a clear argument for the book's place within the larger landscape. But mostly one gets the sense that Watterson is seeing his idol with new eyes, and he marvels at how freely Schulz swiped material from his real life for use in the strip, although always "with a larger human understanding that implicates himself in the sad comedy." Watterson added, "I think that's a wonderfully sane way to process a hurtful world."[61]

These two newspaper stories came out eight years apart, but the contexts in which they appeared were very different. That's because by 2007, the official *Calvin and Hobbes* nostalgia machine was already in high gear. In 2001, the Ohio State University Cartoon Research Library (now called the Billy Ireland Cartoon Library and Museum) contacted Watterson about the possibility of collaborating on an exhibit of his past work. For reasons known only to himself, Watterson agreed, choosing 36 of his favorite Sunday strips, along with their uncolored original drawings and a series of fresh annotations. *Calvin and Hobbes: Sunday Pages 1985–1995* ran from September 2001 to January 2002, and is still easily the most popular show in the museum's history. A catalog from the exhibit was later published as a stand-alone book, including a new essay from Watterson, the opening line of which instantly dashed a thousand hopes for any follow-up strip: "It's been five years since the end of *Calvin and Hobbes*, the longest time in which I haven't drawn cartoons."[62] In the essay, Watterson goes into detail about how his strips were put together technically, as well as the creative liberties that came with the revamped Sunday format. He's also bittersweet about the way the strip's imaginative flights have become commonplace in the ensuing years. "When *Calvin and Hobbes* first appeared, it was somewhat surprising to treat reality as subjective," he writes. "I did this simply as a way to put the reader in Calvin's head and to reveal his imaginative personality. Now these juxtapositions are a visual game for many comic strips, and after all these years, I suspect readers know where this sort of joke is headed as soon as they see it. The novelty cannot be recaptured."[63]

But that exhibition was nothing compared to what was coming down the pipeline. In early 2005, Watterson decided to further secure the strip's legacy by donating his entire *Calvin and Hobbes* archive to the Cartoon Research Library. This included not just the totality of his original artwork (including rare drawings for promotional materials), but also, curiously, all of the original strips Watterson had received over the years from peers like Jim Borgman and Lynn Johnston. Many of these pieces were personally dedicated to Watterson, which makes the move to get rid of them appear all the more cold-blooded. Was there really no room in his life for gifts like these? It was as if Watterson were cutting his entire cartooning era out of his life in one fell swoop.

Later that year, however, the hammer really came down — in the form of a three-volume hardcover box set. If there was any doubt that the strip was finished, the *Complete Calvin and Hobbes* put those arguments to rest. Published by Andrews McMeel, the deluxe box set was the most beautiful and thorough love letter to the strip that fans could have asked for. And they did ask for it: despite a hefty price tag of $150, the set promptly went to number four on the *New York Times* bestseller list. It was one of the most expensive books ever to do so, and — at 23 pounds — the heaviest, full stop. (The paperback edition, for what it's worth, weighs in at a comparatively trim 14.2 pounds.) The set's sheer physicality drew rave reviews, including from the *Times*, where John Hodgman wrote that the collection was "so big and dense and beautifully printed and huge that I have real difficulty carrying it from one room to the next. It is worth the work, and worth every penny."[64] The collection made waves that carried all the way to the comics pages themselves: a *FoxTrot* strip from around the time of the box set's release shows a house from the outside, tilting dramatically to one end. "Peter," a voice from within says, "maybe you should take those *Calvin and Hobbes* books to the other side of the house for a while."

The Complete Calvin and Hobbes lovingly recreated all 3,160 strips, plus the many stand-alone stories and paintings Watterson had drawn for other book collections along the way. It was a meticulous process that took designer Michael Reagan, working in collaboration with an initially reluctant Watterson, more than 18 months to complete. In his acknowledgments, Watterson thanks Reagan for "cheerfully nudging me along," because "as flattering as it is to have a lavish box like this, it can be a little disturbing to see one's own career embalmed in a box."[65] Watterson came around and contributed an all-new ten-page introduction reflecting on his childhood, the strip, and its legacy — hardly the behavior of a world-hating recluse. In it, he also gave readers an exclusive look at some of his early work, including one of the *Raumfahrer Rolf* strips from his high-school German class and early *Calvin and Hobbes* strips where Calvin still has bangs covering his eyes.

It was the final section of Watterson's introduction, however, that held the most promise for those eager to find out what he'd been up to for the past decade. Here, Watterson writes about his growing interest in fine art, which was virtually nonexistent when the strip launched. At first, Watterson wrote, "I liked cartoons because they *weren't* art — they were just funny."[66] Over the years, though, he became more fascinated by their visual possibilities, which you can see in the ambitious, wildly colorful landscapes that pop up more and more often in the later Sunday strips. At a certain point, Watterson's interest in painting overtook his interest in cartooning — which is why he'd spent the previous decade putting his energy into landscape painting, "and a similarly remedial study of music."[67] He readily admitted he was no prodigy in either field, but he relished the challenge, moving from "proficiency and confidence in cartooning to awkwardness and doubt in most everything I do now." As if to prove his point, Watterson included a small oil sketch of a desert landscape that he painted during the final year of *Calvin and Hobbes*. It's pretty. But it's no transmogrifier.

And for those fans still looking for closure, Watterson's introduction went some way to salving their wounded pride. While he still doesn't address his readers directly, Watterson does write that he struggles with having left behind the platform that brought him into millions of homes every morning. "People invest only a few seconds reading any strip, but the cartoonist can talk to readers for years on end, and that's an incredible amount of access to people's minds," he wrote.[68] Watterson is clear that the door to cartooning remains firmly shut. But his closing sentence strikes a far warmer note than anything in 1995's farewell letter: "I truly loved drawing this comic strip, and I'll always look back on *Calvin and Hobbes* with great pride and affection."[69]

You might think that, having given the strip its big final send-off, Watterson was now free to disappear from public life entirely. His past behavior would certainly suggest this was his goal. In reality, however, the reverse happened: Watterson began to gradually pop up more and more often. In fact, since 2010, hardly a year has passed without some kind of new appearance from the supposed recluse, often in places and contexts that literally nobody would have expected.

In 2010, Watterson's hometown paper, the *Cleveland Plain Dealer*, decided to celebrate the 25th anniversary of *Calvin and Hobbes*, publishing not only a retrospective article about the strip and its legacy, but also an all-new Q&A with Watterson himself — his first media appearance since the ill-fated *L.A. Times* story some 20 years earlier. Then, he did *another* one, with the magazine *Mental Floss* in 2013. (Even the *MF* editor in chief has admitted he had no idea why Watterson agreed to their request.) The fact of these interviews' existence was one thing, but it was even more relieving to see Watterson come off as eloquent as ever — if still occasionally prickly — on the page. On the subject of grieving fans, he said, "This isn't as hard to understand as people try to make it. By the end of ten years, I'd said pretty much everything I had come there to say." Watterson pointed out that he wrote *Calvin and Hobbes* in his 30s, and that he was "many miles from there" now. "An artwork can stay frozen in time," he added, "but I stumble through the years like everyone else. I think the deeper fans understand that, and are willing to give me some room to go on with my life."[70]

Words were one thing. But it was something else entirely when it was revealed that, after 16 years of retirement, Watterson had at long last produced a new piece of comic art. The *Washington Post* reported in 2011 that a brand-new 6" x 8" oil painting of a character from Richard Thompson's strip *Cul de Sac* would be included in a new anthology raising money for Parkinson's research. (Thompson was diagnosed with Parkinson's in 2009, and passed away in 2016 due to complications from the disease.) Watterson was friendly with Thompson, but the new painting was more than anyone had expected. "Let's just say I got a package from a William Watterson . . ." said an editor at Andrews McMeel at the time. "I have been carrying it around and showing everyone. I didn't get my hopes up that he would contribute . . ."[71]

Then, in 2014, it happened again. Watterson agreed to draw a poster for the Angoulême International Comics Festival, where he had been awarded the Grand Prix the year before, and even did another short Q&A with the free French daily newspaper *20 Minutes*. That same year, Watterson designed the poster for the American documentary *Stripped*, about the changing face of newspaper cartooning. Even more noteworthy is that Watterson actually appears in the film — or at least his voice does, in what the directors claim is the first audio interview he's ever agreed to. "I certainly found drawing a comic strip consuming work," Watterson says in the film. "I had virtually no life beyond the drawing board. But I wasn't looking for a balanced life in those days. My comic strip was the way that I explored the world and my own perceptions and thoughts. So to switch off the job, I would've had to switch off my head. Yes, the work was insanely intense, but that was the whole point of doing it."[72]

Still, the holy grail for Watterson fans was always a return to his old stomping grounds: the daily newspaper comics page. Incredibly, in 2014 they got that, too. And even more incredibly, almost nobody spotted it when it happened.

For years, Stephan Pastis had used his strip *Pearls Before Swine* to mock his own limitations as an artist. The three-part story that ran in papers over June 4–6, 2014, was no exception: a second-grader named Libby shows up at Pastis's door and decides she can do a better job illustrating the strip than he can — and then proceeds to do just that.

The strips were funny, but to careful readers, Libby's clearly superior drawing style raised an eyebrow. Who, exactly, was drawing these panels? In a blog post published the next day, Pastis dropped the bomb: it was Watterson. Now 19 years after leaving the funny pages behind, he had returned, uncredited, and camouflaging himself within someone else's strip. It turned out that a few months earlier, Pastis had been in touch with Watterson, who mentioned that he had an idea for Pastis's strip. "Now if you had asked me the odds of Bill Watterson saying that line to me," Pastis wrote on his blog, "I'd say it had about the same likelihood of Jimi Hendrix telling me he had a new guitar riff. And yes, I'm aware Hendrix is dead."[73] It was Watterson's idea to keep their collaboration a secret until the strips ran, and Pastis's blog post suggests that that restraint basically brought him to the edge of spontaneous combustion. The following day's *Pearls Before Swine* had Pastis giving a final tip of the hat to Watterson, as the precocious Libby dons full snow gear, despite it being the height of summer, and says she has to leave because "there's a magical world out there to explore." (Fittingly, the dopey Pastis character doesn't get the reference.)

Watterson has made other, intermittent appearances in recent years, from writing forewords for other cartoonists' books, to holding a joint art show with Richard Thompson, to, most intriguingly, providing a logo and a series of scratch-board drawings for a flamenco rock opera created by fellow Clevelander Ethan Margolis. "I think the pressure for him to be associated so much with Calvin has been reduced a little bit," Salem says, which allows Watterson to follow his nose when it comes to new projects. "If he gets something in his vision that he really likes, then he'll reach out."[74]

But the most significant work Watterson has been part of, post-retirement, has to be *Exploring Calvin and Hobbes*, another lavish catalog created to accompany a second exhibit of the cartoonist's work at the Billy Ireland museum, and published in book form in 2015. The materials from the exhibit are interesting in their own right, but the crown jewel of the book is an extended interview between Watterson and museum curator Jenny Robb. Lively, charming, and more intimate and wide-ranging than any that had come before it, this will, said the *Washington Post*, "likely long stand as the definitive Bill Watterson interview."[75]

Perhaps because of his pre-existing relationship with Robb and the museum, Watterson sounds loose and less guarded than ever. For the first time, he really opens up about his struggles, like the time he had a meltdown about scheduling and needed his wife to help him get out from behind the eight ball. Watterson chats about his love of Old Master painters and German woodcuts alike. And he takes pleasure in popping the occasional bubble about *Calvin and Hobbes* lore: when asked whether his family was religious growing up, Watterson says no. "So, on the assumption that you're leading up to why I named my central character after a 16th-century theologian . . . well, it was a joke. *(laughter)* Mostly on me."[76]

It's especially difficult to read this conversation and come away with the notion of Watterson as any kind of bitter recluse. "The attention makes me very self-conscious and wary of people's motives, so I find the whole thing enervating," Watterson says at one point. "Maybe there would've been a smarter way to handle it, but I couldn't think of it, and this seemed to be what I had to do. It was sort of a no-win scenario, and just one of the most bizarre aspects of my job."[77] In many ways, *Exploring Calvin and Hobbes* is the perfect final entry in the strip's life — the keystone that stabilizes the rest of the arch for good. It also contains the only bit of reflection from Watterson about his audience that you'll ever need to read:

> BW: One of the beauties of a comic strip is that people's expectations are nil. If you draw anything more subtle than a pie in the face,

you're considered a philosopher. You can sneak in an honest reflection once in a while, because readers rarely have their guard up.

I love the unpretentiousness of cartoons. If you sat down and wrote a 200-page book called *My Big Thoughts on Life*, no one would read it. But if you stick those same thoughts in a comic strip and wrap them in a little joke that takes five seconds to read, now you're talking to millions. Any writer would kill for that kind of audience. What a gift.

JR: Is that something you miss? Having that opportunity?

BW: Yes, I do miss that.[78]

In the years since *Calvin and Hobbes* disappeared from newspapers, with no follow-up to speak of, many have been tempted to peg Watterson himself as a kind of anti-Calvin: someone whose imagination simply dried up. In fact, he appears to have achieved the opposite. When his comic was in its prime, Watterson held true to the vision in his head — a vision that almost nobody else could see, let alone understand — and this despite financial and commercial temptations that most of us could only dream of. Later, as his attention began to wander, he was able to continue his career, again on his own terms. Like Calvin, Watterson had plans that didn't make sense to a lot of people. But they made sense to him, and that's what mattered. "It's pretty clear his mind is going in a whole lot of different artistic directions," Salem says. "To my knowledge, he's doing a lot of artwork, but none of it is in comic form. Alas, I think those days are behind him."[79]

Where does that leave Watterson's fans? On the one hand, the barriers between audiences and creators have never been lower, which has led to increased communication as well as heightened, and often unclear, expectations. "It's a weird kind of dance," says Brad Guigar, creator of the webcomic *Evil Inc.*, in the documentary *Stripped*. "Because you want [readers] to be invested. You want them to be fully part of what you're doing. And at the same time, there's only so far you can go."[80] This overall ease of access makes Watterson's refusal to engage all the more keenly felt. At the same time, nobody could accuse him of misleading his readers. The deal, from very early on, was that he gave you *Calvin and Hobbes*, and nothing else. The strip was it. And the strip was supposed to be enough. "Quite honestly, I tried to forget that there *was* an audience," Watterson says in *Stripped*. "I wanted to keep the strip feeling small and intimate as I did it. So my goal was just to make my wife laugh. After that, I put it out and the public could take it or leave it."[81]

So, really, how can there be a book called *Looking for Calvin and Hobbes*, as if we don't already have it? How can there be a film called *Dear Mr. Watterson*, as if a fan's love for the work is only real if the cartoonist receives it personally?

Watterson has even addressed the idea of closure within a work of art from the other side, as a fan. Back in 1999, in that first post–*C&H* article for the *Los Angeles Times*, Watterson wrote about the influence *Peanuts* had had on him as a kid, and his sadness at the strip coming to an end after being a reliable, comforting presence in the newspaper all these years. "Schulz has given all his readers a great gift," Watterson wrote, "and my gratitude for that tempers my disappointment at the strip's cessation."[82]

Ultimately, anyone looking for closure need look no further than the strip itself. "I would hope they look at his last [strip] as closure," Salem says. "Calvin and Hobbes sailing off into the snow, and saying, 'Let's go exploring!' I think he looked on that as something new in his life, and I think it was meant for readers, too. Let's all move on in different directions, together."[83]

5

Imagine a Six-Year-Old Peeing on the Ford Logo — Forever

When the dust had settled, it became clear that all of Watterson's conflicts with his syndicate — the renegotiation of ownership rights, the revamped Sunday strips, the extended sabbaticals, the reflexive refusal of all licensing requests — could be boiled down to one thing: control. As the strip's sole creator, he wanted to retain as much artistic command as possible during its run, letting the characters, rather than the so-called *Calvin and Hobbes* brand, dictate future storylines. He wanted to keep the corrosive effects of merchandising as far away from the work itself as possible. And he wanted, in both the business and creative realms, to be the only cook in the kitchen. Of all his gripes with the cartooning industry, none was stronger than Watterson's disapproval of cartoonists using assistants, and of strips being carried on, under syndicate control, after the creator's retirement or death. "I spent five years trying to get this stupid job and now that I have it I'm not going to hire it out to somebody else," he told *Honk* magazine back in 1987. "I'm willing to take the blame if the strip goes down the drain, and I want the credit if it succeeds. So long as it has my name on it, I want it to be mine."[84]

It's incredible how close Watterson came to achieving this goal. After signing a restrictive entry-level contract in 1985, Watterson waited until the strip's popularity became undeniable, then leveraged his power with the syndicate to make sure nobody else could take his characters away from him. Then the strip stopped on a dime because he didn't feel like making it anymore. And while it isn't true that *Calvin and Hobbes* was *never* licensed — recall the wall calendars and the children's textbook — when you consider the mind-bogglingly lucrative offers he received, as well as the general eagerness among his peers to cash in at their first opportunity, it's nothing short of miraculous that the strip has survived all these years with its image intact. Today, if you want to experience *Calvin and Hobbes*, your only way to do so is to return to the strips themselves — the individual collections, the commentary-filled *Tenth Anniversary Book*, and the deluxe, lovingly prepared *Complete Calvin and Hobbes* box set. There are no cheap plastic toys cluttering up eBay, and no lukewarm animated miniseries gathering dust in the DVD clearance bin. All told, Watterson's strip has a remarkable legacy of artistic purity.

OK, except for that one thing.

You know the one.

Some origin stories are forever lost to the mists of time. Sadly, we'll never know who was the first person to read *Calvin and Hobbes* on June 5, 1988, and think, "Hey, in that one part, Calvin looks like he's peeing." But whoever that individual was, they couldn't have known that this one stray (and kinda weird) thought would one day lead to a massive, lucrative, and completely illegal cottage industry. Because on that day, the Peeing Calvin was born. The back windows of pickup trucks would never be the same.

To see a Peeing Calvin decal today is to experience a moment of confusion: *Wait, did Watterson actually draw Calvin urinating?* So much time has passed that it's understandable for fans not to have every last strip memorized. But no. Watterson didn't draw it, and he certainly didn't authorize it. The strip in question is a summertime Sunday about water balloons. In the fourth panel, we see Calvin hunched over a tap around the side of his house, holding a purple balloon up to the spout while turning the handle with his other hand.

Here's the thing, though: no matter how you look at this panel, Calvin . . . doesn't really look like he's peeing. His back is turned, and he's grinning mischievously, sure. And the "FWOOOOSH" sound effect running across the top has a vaguely urinous connotation, I suppose. But both of Calvin's hands are visible. There is nothing that could even remotely be mistaken for a stream of pee anywhere on the panel. And most importantly, he's clearly doing something else. Calvin once asked Hobbes, "Who was the guy who first looked at a cow and said, 'I think I'll drink whatever comes out of these things when I squeeze 'em?'" We might ask something similar about this panel. Of all the mysteries surrounding the rise of the Peeing Calvin, perhaps the most perplexing is how it got started in the first place.*

But start it did. The Peeing Calvin turned out to be a perfect fit for the kind of messaging that a certain segment of North Americans love to slap on the backs of their vehicles. To wit: the Peeing Calvin is (a) a recognizable character (b) doing something outrageous that (c) easily and "cleverly" demonstrates the owner's hatred of any logo, person, or concept. And all it took was a few minor adjustments to Watterson's original drawing. Gone are the tap and the balloon. Calvin's pants have been lowered to mid-cheek level, and a new sort of half-arm has been added, angled toward his groin, along with the critical arc of pee itself. Most important is the splash point, which gives the decals their versatility, allowing Calvin to aim his urine-based dismissal at any cause under the sun.

The first known appearance of the decal was on November 26, 1995, when a reporter noted a Peeing Calvin on the side of a motor home in Florida, urinating onto the letters *FSU*. This was a reference to the ongoing football rivalry between Florida State University and the University of Florida; presumably the owner was more of a UF person. From there, the sightings quickly multiplied, with newspapers in cities across the American South recording more and more of these

---

* In fact, it isn't even fully settled which strip was the origin point. Most *Calvin* fans peg the June 5, 1988, strip as the culprit — but in another Sunday strip a year later, Watterson drew what is basically the exact same panel: same pose, same grin, even the same sound effect. Could *this* strip, in fact, be the true origin of the Peeing Calvin?

bootleg decals, many tied up in the world of sports, with its almost tribal sense of loyalty. And the people who sold them were aggressively anti-Wattersonian in their desire to profit off Calvin's back, even though the decals were crass, and clearly illegal. As one merchant who specialized in stickers of Calvin peeing on the numbers of various NASCAR drivers told the *Chicago Tribune*, "I think it's disgusting, but who am I to say it?"[85]

The Peeing Calvin may have been an effective way to get one's message across, but it quickly drew the ire of law enforcement. In 1996, a woman in South Carolina was given an obscenity warning by the highway patrol for her decal of Calvin peeing on the letters *IRS*. This story became a national curio, making it the first time most Americans caught wind of what had been, up to that point, a regional phenomenon. It also became the unlikely grounds for a First Amendment battle, as the American Civil Liberties Union announced it would defend the woman, along with another South Carolinian who had been busted for his own Peeing Calvin, on the grounds that a urinating cartoon character did not, in fact, meet the definition of obscenity.

Not that some within law enforcement didn't see the decals' appeal. That same year, a sheriff in Florida's Duval County suspended one of his officers and gave another a written reprimand for sticking Peeing Calvins onto the backs of their personal vehicles — an act that the pair might have gotten away with, had these particular Calvins not been urinating onto the sheriff's name, alongside a star representing his badge.

Once the South Carolina case made national headlines, the Peeing Calvin's popularity reached a new fever pitch. Because the decals are made by a number of small, unconnected companies, it's impossible to map exactly how they spread across the continent, or to chart the many variations that have popped up over the years. Phil Edwards, writing for the website *Trivia Happy*, found likenesses of Calvin peeing on everything from *CITY BOYS* to *LAWYERS* to *MY EX*,[86] and a cursory internet search adds more topical references like *ISIS* and *OBAMA*. Some of these companies, perhaps mindful of Watterson's intellectual property, have borrowed the pose but changed the Calvin figure to a more generic little boy, a squatting female figure, or, in some cases, an alien (I don't know, either). There's even an oddly serious, urine-free subset where Calvin is on his knees, praying in front of a large cross.

The most common target for Calvin's wrath, however, is truck companies. The Ford/Chevy debate is a long-standing point of contention among American truck drivers. But the Peeing Calvin suddenly made that debate a lot more visible, especially to those confused parties who just happened to be stuck behind one of the partisans in traffic. "The P-Calvin," as Hank Stuever called it, writing for the *Austin American Statesman* in 1999, "skirts a fine line between macho pride and the early stages of road rage." Stuever tried to interview Peeing Calvin owners for a think piece about what the decals meant for the state of American culture, with mixed results: most of the gruff men he approached "[told] me, more or less, to go truck myself."[87]

Stuever claims that the Peeing Calvin is, in essence, the new gun rack. "Which is to say," he writes, "the beefing up of gun control in America has forced certain males of particular demographics" — rednecks, basically — "to seek new visual codes to explain their concise yet overlooked worldview(s)." That perceived underdog status is key, agrees Mike Preston, a professor at the University of Colorado in Boulder. "It's a distinctly bottom-of-the-pyramid type of humor," he told the Colorado Springs *Gazette* in 2004. "You see Calvin sprinkling 'my job,' but not 'my employees.' This is a way for these people to feel empowered, which they may not be able to do at work or home."[88] In that sense, the Peeing Calvin's illegality might actually make it *more* appealing to its clientele: another small way of sticking it to the man.

It's not like Watterson or his syndicate are able to do much about it, anyway. Even though Peeing Calvin decals are still sold in broad daylight, Universal Press Syndicate has decided it isn't worth the effort to enforce its copyright on such small-potatoes operations. "If we see it happening with the stickers, then the attorneys can start their thing," Kathie Kerr, then the syndicate's director of communications, said in 1999.[89] "But these are sort of fly-by-night operators. It moves around a lot, so you never really catch anyone."

Ironically, it's Watterson's hard-line anti-merchandising stance that may be partly to blame for the proliferation of the Peeing Calvin in the first place. Kerr says that when the cartoonist vetoed attempts to license the strip, that decision "eliminated some of the watchdogs . . . When you license a character, then you increase the number of attorneys who keep a lookout and protect the images."[90]

The Peeing Calvin doesn't appear to be going anywhere anytime soon. And who knows? Maybe that's for the best. An article in the satirical newspaper *The Onion* once declared the Peeing Calvin a "vital part of our national dialogue, used by millions of Americans to exchange viewpoints and ideas about the important issues of the day."[91] This is obviously a joke more about the diminished state of American discourse than about the decal itself, but the fact that the writers chose the Peeing Calvin is proof of the symbol's ubiquity, as well as how well the decals have cornered that particular market. Clearly, the Peeing Calvin has marked its territory. While undeniably juvenile, it was nonetheless the first time a part of *Calvin and Hobbes* transcended the confines of the strip and reinvented itself to find a home in corners of society that even Watterson couldn't have reached on his own. As he admitted in 2013, "I figure that, long after the strip is gone, those decals are my ticket to immortality."[92]

Watterson may be right that the Peeing Calvin will live on after some have forgotten the source. But when it comes to continuing the legacy of *Calvin and Hobbes*, there are plenty of other, more explicit successors to Watterson's throne to choose from. These tributes to *C&H* exist at various points along the spectrum between homage and fan fiction, and show that the imagination that once fueled Calvin's world isn't dead

— it's just been transferred to his readers, many of whom grew up to make Watterson-influenced art of their own.

These tributes started to pop up as the strip approached the end of its run, and one particular early farewell became a leading fan theory about how Calvin's adventures might wrap up. "However Watterson chooses to end *Calvin and Hobbes*, there is really only one end," wrote *Washington Post* staffer Frank Ahrens on November 19, 1995. "It will live in my brain forever, if not on the newspaper page."[93] Ahrens goes on to describe an imagined final Sunday strip where Calvin and Hobbes build a snowman together. At one point, Calvin hears a noise, and Hobbes tells him, "It's just your imagination." Calvin turns away to continue working on the snowman, and when he turns back, he sees Hobbes sitting there. But it isn't the Hobbes he usually sees. Instead, Hobbes is now "small and stuffed," with "short, blunted paws and button eyes. He [is] slumped forward in the snow, flaccid, lifeless." In other words, Calvin's unique version of reality will finally give way to the one that everyone else sees. Calvin will blink, confused, and then walk away, leaving his best friend behind forever.

Ahrens wouldn't be the last to want closure from *Calvin and Hobbes*, especially when it came to finally resolving the question of Hobbes's reality, and his proposed solution would have certainly accomplished that, however unsubtly. And his idea has shown legs in the years since, even leading to a conspiracy theory about a supposedly "lost" final *C&H* strip showing a variation on Ahrens's suggested finale, where Hobbes reverts to plush as a result of some new pills Calvin has been prescribed to improve his concentration. There are several drawn versions of this strip floating around online, none particularly convincing. But their pursuit of a clear resolution to the strip's central ambiguity — as well as their use of heavy medication to get there — is a theme that would be picked up by many others in subsequent years.

Generally, tributes to *Calvin and Hobbes* fall into two different categories: imagining Calvin's life post-strip, or looking at his existing adventures through a new lens. Several of Watterson's peers, from Bill Amend (*FoxTrot*), to Darby Conley (*Get Fuzzy*), to Berkeley Breathed (*Bloom County*), snuck Calvin and Hobbes cameos into their strips over the years, either to riff on their place in the comics pantheon, or else to suggest that these characters were, in fact, still running around and causing mischief in the larger, ongoing universe that all cartoons inhabit. Steve Troop's webcomic *Mayberry Melonpool* included multiple homages to Watterson's strip, including a story where one character discovers Calvin, along with figures from other beloved canceled strips, living on and playing poker together in a kind of secret cartoon no man's land. Other strips simply showed characters reading *Calvin and Hobbes* in the newspaper, as if there were a happier alternate dimension where Watterson never discovered landscape painting. There was something undeniably soothing about seeing Opus poring over a Sunday *C&H* with a bowl of cereal, or *FoxTrot*'s Andy reading what appeared to be a new sledding strip.

In 2016, Breathed took his well-known love of the strip a step further, announcing that Calvin and Hobbes were returning to newspapers — for good! — and joining the cast of his revived *Bloom County*. A sample strip showed the duo back to their old tricks, with Hobbes threatening to eat Opus. Better still, Breathed announced a line of *C&H* merchandise at long last, including winter hats and a branded pasta strainer. "Watterson's in great shape," Breathed wrote on his Facebook page as the news broke. "He's out of the Arizona facility, continent and looking forward to some well-earned financial security."[94] Oh, and the date of this too-good-to-be-true announcement? April 1.

Of course, straightforward homage tends not to be as funny as something with a little more bite to it. So, more often, a cartoonist's tribute to *Calvin and Hobbes* would include a twist on the existing characters, and the majority of these reached for the low-hanging fruit that was Calvin's mental state. Watterson always maintained that his six-year-old hero simply saw Hobbes differently than everyone else did. But it isn't hard to imagine a psychiatrist observing this behavior and then reaching for her prescription pad. Enter strips like Mark Parisi's *Off the Mark*, which on different occasions showed Calvin in a mental hospital, recovering from "tiger hallucinations," and later staring dead-eyed at the reader as a result of taking antipsychotic drugs. (Parisi seems more interested than most in Calvin's post-strip fate; two days after the *Calvin and Hobbes* finale, Parisi drew a stuffed Hobbes with a huge stomach, while in the distance Calvin's mom asks his dad, "Did you just hear a burp?" The caption at the bottom reads "What really happened to Calvin.") The stop-motion sketch comedy show *Robot Chicken* took a similar tack in its 2006 parody of the strip, in which Calvin murders his parents with a chainsaw and then blames it on his stuffed tiger. I suppose I'd recommend this segment to anyone who's a fan of six-year-olds getting electroshock therapy. But that's about it.

An even more morbid fascination with Calvin's post-strip life can be found in the work of Mark Tatulli, whose strip *Lio* included a story where the title character, a young boy himself, discovers Calvin's corpse in the snow. The implication is that after charging off down the hill with Hobbes in that iconic final strip, he immediately crashed and died. From there, Lio manages to resurrect Calvin, who then spends several strips chasing after him until Lio is finally able to trap him inside a copy of (what else?) *The Complete Calvin and Hobbes*. This story was later collected in *There's Corpses Everywhere*, a dark twist on Watterson's *There's Treasure Everywhere*. On the cover, Lio is shown once again digging up Calvin's skull and abandoned tiger doll. Tatulli even recreates that famous photograph of Watterson for his own author photo, right down to the sweater and glasses. "*Calvin and Hobbes* is sort of this sacred cow among comic strips that others dare not touch," Tatulli explained to the *Washington Post* in 2010. "And there's nothing I like more than skewering a sacred cow."[95] Interestingly, Tatulli shares a publisher with Watterson, and executives at Andrews McMeel and Universal initially balked at releasing a book that took such gruesome aim at their flagship property. Which only egged the hornet's nest–poking Tatulli on further: "Finding out my publisher was against it really convinced me I wanted to do it."

Watterson's strip also had plenty to offer the next generation of cartoonists on a technical level. Many creators, including Parisi, Chari Pere, and *Stone Soup*'s Jan Eliot, have credited Watterson's over-the-top facial expressions as an inspiration for their own work. "Watterson brought back that exaggeration without making it plastic," Parisi told author Nevin Martell.[96] Others have zeroed in on the way he drew trees, hands, and even water. Mark Tatulli, meanwhile, has said that he first got the idea of using a brush in his cartoons when he realized that's what Watterson did.

More broadly, the structure of Calvin's fantasies has become just another part of the comics page's shared language, to the point that you can now find fantasy sequences that suddenly revert back to reality in the final panel in strips like *Zits*. The most common refrain from Watterson's peers and successors, however, is that he never used those constant daily deadlines as an excuse to turn in subpar work. "For Bill, it wasn't enough to just meet the deadline," says *FoxTrot* creator Bill Amend. "You had to move the bar a little bit [higher] over what you'd done previously."[97] The world of *Calvin and Hobbes* was large enough, and detailed enough, to suggest something to just about everyone who followed in its footsteps. "It's probably hard to name a comic-strip artist who came along from the 1990s onward who wasn't influenced in some way by *Calvin and Hobbes*," says Andrew Farago, curator of San Francisco's Cartoon Art Museum.[98]

Outside the world of newspaper comics, tributes to *Calvin and Hobbes* are just as widespread. Animated TV shows like

Family Guy have made knowing winks to the characters, and comic books like *Spencer and Locke* (which bills itself as "*Calvin and Hobbes* meets *Sin City*") have also tried updating Watterson's dynamic for a more adult audience, to match the age of fans of the original strip, who are all now in their 30s and beyond. Brothers Dan and Tom Heyerman, meanwhile, used their webcomic *Pants Are Overrated* to test out a miniseries called *Hobbes and Bacon*, in which an adult Calvin passes Hobbes down to his six-year-old daughter, thus starting the cycle of adventure anew. This miniseries, which drew praise from NPR's Robert Krulwich, among others, is notable both for the accuracy and warmth of its drawings and for how well-adjusted it portrays the adult Calvin being. (It doesn't hurt that he's married to Susie Derkins, who has grown to share Calvin's love of gross-out humor — to the frowning disapproval of both Bacon and Hobbes.) And YouTube is chockablock with amateur animators who've tried to reverentially bring the strip to life, perhaps in the way that Watterson might have imagined back when he admitted to the *Comics Journal* that of all the ways the strip could be licensed, animation was the one he hated the least. Writer and musician Rafael Casal went the other way, shooting a live-action web series called *Hobbes & Me* — co-starring a pre-*Hamilton* Daveed Diggs as Hobbes — that recreated well-known strips, frame by frame and line by line; one review described it as "like getting a hug from a tiger, in a good way."[99]

The list of *Calvin and Hobbes* tributes is long, and growing steadily. But of all the successors to date, the one that comes

closest to capturing the spirit of the strip and its legacy —
written from the perspective not of a peer, but of a fan — is a
Canadian young-adult novel set in small-town Ontario.

Martine Leavitt's *Calvin* was published in 2015, and went
on to win that year's Governor General's Literary Award
for young people's literature in the text category. It's about
a boy named Calvin, his neighbor/crush/nemesis Susie, and
a bipedal tiger that only Calvin can see — and if you squint
hard enough, you might be able to convince yourself that it's
like Watterson's strip never left. In reality, Calvin is a socially
awkward 17-year-old living in the town of Leamington, on the
northern shore of Lake Erie. Susie is an aspiring writer who
has abandoned him to date their school's version of Moe (here
renamed Maurice). And Hobbes? Well, this Calvin *did* used
to have a stuffed tiger when he was younger, until one day it
fell apart after a particularly rough trip through the washing
machine. And from that day on, something important changed
inside Calvin's mind:

> After Hobbes died, I wasn't scared of the monsters
> under the bed anymore. I started to be afraid of cli-
> mate change and nuclear bombs and all the things I
> heard on the news that didn't go shrinking away when
> you turned on the light or your mom walked into
> the room.
>
> Now I was 17 and a tiger was talking to me and
> I wasn't scared of the monsters under the bed. I was
> scared of the monster *in* the bed, which was me.[100]

In other words, when Calvin's stuffed tiger died, his imagination went with it. (Though it should be said that his cartoon namesake already had an interest in things like protecting the environment; see, for instance, the title story from *Yukon Ho!*) But as the novel opens, Hobbes makes a sudden re-emergence in Calvin's life — not as his cuddly best friend, but as a menacing, uncontrollable creature always lurking just out of sight. Everyone who hears about the case is in agreement: Calvin has schizophrenia.

So far we've got basically the same premise as a throwaway *Robot Chicken* joke. But Leavitt's novel distinguishes itself in a couple of important ways. First, with its raw and complex portrayal of mental illness: from the outset, Calvin knows he's sick ("I'm too old for an imaginary friend," he whispers when Hobbes first reveals himself[101]), and he's frantic to find a way to get better. Second, in the details of its inventive plot: Calvin convinces himself that the only way to be cured is to walk to Cleveland — across Lake Erie, in the dead of winter — to see Bill Watterson, who he believes will present him with a brand-new, never-before-seen *Calvin and Hobbes* strip showing his child protagonist as a healthy teenager who doesn't need his stuffed tiger anymore. This, Calvin is convinced, will banish the Hobbes in his head back into his own childhood, where he belongs. So he sends emails to Andrews McMeel Publishing and the *Cleveland Plain Dealer*, in the hopes of alerting Watterson to his trip; the book we're reading is presented as a third letter, addressed to Bill himself.

But the way *Calvin* really sets itself apart is by positioning itself not as a continuation of Watterson's strip, but rather a by-product of its conclusion. We learn early on that Calvin's birthday happens to be December 31, 1995, a date that takes on added significance once Hobbes reappears. "It was possible something cosmic was happening here," he thinks. "Maybe Calvin was so real to so many people that on the day I was born, which was the day the last *Calvin and Hobbes* comic came out, maybe all that love and sadness people felt . . . I opened up my mouth to get my first breath, and I just sucked it in." He concludes, "I wasn't sick. I was Calvin come to life!"[102]

Leavitt is thus channeling two different phenomena here. On the one hand is the strip itself, as she repurposes familiar tropes like Spaceman Spiff and the deranged mutant killer monster snow goons to reflect this Calvin's troubled mental state. But at the same time, her novel directly riffs on the experience of Watterson's frustrated fans, and she transforms that feeling into something much larger. Her Calvin is a direct, and possibly literal, result of all that "love and sadness" that had nowhere to go once Watterson pulled the plug on the strip. And maybe, Calvin suggests to Susie, "Once you create an idea and millions of people are loving that idea, when you get brilliance and love all mixed up like that, it makes something that has to go somewhere. It impacts reality, like a meteorite hitting Earth. Bang! I think the universe just couldn't let Calvin go."[103] It's a nice idea, and one that certainly flatters the perspective of fans who felt their grief went unheard and unappreciated by the strip's creator; if Watterson wasn't listening, then *the universe itself* would do it for him, and respond in kind.

Once Calvin tells Susie his plan, he's shocked when she announces that she's coming with him. From here, the novel takes on a surreal, almost magical quality. Calvin becomes convinced that Susie, too, is an illusion; why else would this beautiful, popular girl risk her life for the weirdo down the street? Things only get wilder once they actually reach the lake. The duo (plus Hobbes, still lurking) ends up encountering a series of people as they trudge across the ice, and it turns out each one of them has a connection to Bill Watterson: the fisherman who cried when the strip ended; the bearded poet who met him once, years earlier. Calvin and Susie, pouncing on the potential cosmic significance, push the poet for details but are rebuffed. "You want me to say something particular," the man says, "something that will make him seem realer than he was before. But he's just a man, a mediocre fisherman who likes a poem once in a while."[104] To anyone who's followed the strip's legacy, this is familiar language. Like all those who have set out in search of Watterson over the years, Calvin and Susie seem doomed to be disappointed — or worse.

Calvin operates on these multiple levels for the rest of its runtime, blending a classic quest narrative (with Watterson serving as the absent father/God figure), a coming-of-age tale, and a teenage love story, with a steady supply of Easter eggs for die-hard fans of the strip thrown in for good measure. Let's just say that any writer who name-drops Lee Salem in her YA book is not messing around. Leavitt's Calvin has more than a little in common with Don Quixote, driven mad by reading too many stories, his mental state now inexorably tangled up in the material that pushed him over the edge. Yet in *Calvin*, that fuzzy line of reality is blurred even further, as his Sancho Panza might *also* be a figment of his imagination. It would certainly explain why Susie, a casual fan, is now able to recite Watterson's birthday, the names of his family members, and even obscure *C&H* trivia (like the Calvin character's original name, Marvin) without hesitation.

By explicitly setting her novel in the post–*Calvin and Hobbes* world, Leavitt provides the best articulation we have to date of how one can continue and even add to, rather than diminish, the spirit of the original strip. Like Watterson's Calvin, hers struggles with the intersection of reality and imagination. He has lately become interested in the workings of the brain, which leads him to declare that so-called real life is just "this game people play together, something your brain decides on, and the minute your brain gets iffy about reality, they realize everything they know about the world is just their own made-up version of it."[105] At the same time, Calvin does seem to lead something of a charmed life. When a truck with no doors or roof comes barreling toward him and Susie, hours into their hike, in search of someone named Fred, Calvin says, "Sometimes the world is crazier than me." To which Susie replies, quietly, "Stuff like that only happens when I'm with you."[106] Out on the ice, without the neat delineation of Watterson's fantasy strips — where the final panel always serves as the border between imagination and Calvin's actual life — there's no way to tell what's real and what is pretend.

As the pair make their way across the lake, falling behind

on their original timeline and running dangerously low on food, Calvin is forced to confront the limits of his imagination, especially as it relates to mental illness. "Maybe the loneliest feeling in the world, Bill," he writes, "is the feeling you get when you see something no one else can see, or hear something no one else can hear, or believe something no one else can believe. Maybe that's the worst thing about what I have, that alone feeling, knowing that I can't make anyone really understand about Hobbes."[107] And here, finally, the two worlds collide. In this moment, Leavitt's Calvin *is* Watterson's Calvin, finally able to describe the ambient sadness that surrounded his childhood in a way that he never could as a six-year-old. What was once the best part of young Calvin's life has become the worst part for his teenaged self. This is what his Uncle Max saw coming, once upon a time, and what he warned Calvin's mom about, to no avail. Calvin never tried to build a social network because for a long time he didn't think he needed one. Now, with even his imaginary friend turning on him, Calvin realizes just how alone he really is.

But rather than simply medicate Calvin into normalcy, as the two-bit version of this story might have it, Leavitt again finds a subtler way to thread the needle, letting Calvin's imagination and mental illness work themselves out in dramatic fashion in the book's climax. While drawing on many of Watterson's imaginative tropes over the course of the novel, Leavitt's Calvin also imagines a character who never appeared in the strip: a terrifying sea creature named Jenny Greenteeth, who lives beneath the lake's surface and finally emerges from a crack in the ice just as Calvin and Susie are at their weakest. After all these years, now hopelessly lost in the middle of Lake Erie in what was, from the beginning, a kind of suicide mission, Calvin is finally at the mercy of his own mind — and that's when Hobbes steps in, figuratively and literally, walking directly into Calvin's field of vision for the first time, to defend his erstwhile best friend. Leavitt has said in interviews that this confrontation draws on scientific research about how schizophrenia manifests itself and how it can be managed. But in the heat of the moment, this scene feels just as much about restoring the relationship that is the very heart of not just Watterson's strip, but the many imitators, descendants, and homage-payers that have come in its wake. After spending the entire novel pacing menacingly in the background, Hobbes finally steps out from the shadows and chooses a side.

Bill Watterson doesn't have much time for legacies. He's always maintained that, for him, the strip has been dead and buried since January 1, 1996, the morning a *Calvin and Hobbes*–sized hole first appeared in newspapers around the world after providing a decade of reliable company. Since then, whenever an interviewer has gotten close enough to put the question to him, he always demurs: it's up to the public now. And however they judge the strip, it's their call to make. He's on to other things.

With so much supplemental material out there, not to mention the *Complete Calvin and Hobbes* box sets standing sentry on so many bookshelves, fans of the strip have more than enough to placate themselves. They may never get that definitive *Calvin and Hobbes* movie, or TV show, or plush doll. But they did get a sustained work of comic art that was about as true to its creator's vision as we will ever see in the mainstream newspaper syndicate system. As for the sting of having their favorite comic disappear so quickly? Well, it's been 20 years. And that sting has gradually lessened and transformed into some grade-A comics lore, a story for fans to bond over and revisit, in depth and at length, at conventions, in bars, or online, together. A piece of art only truly disappears when people stop talking about it. *Calvin and Hobbes* is at no such risk.

Readers of the strip may also take solace in Watterson's own words. In one of the strip's final Sunday editions, on October 15, 1995, Calvin and Hobbes are walking through the woods, debating the merits of fall. Hobbes loves it. But Calvin finds the whole season "melancholy" because it's all just a reminder that summer is gone, and winter is on its way. To which Hobbes responds, "If good things lasted forever, how would we appreciate how precious they are?"

At the time, readers couldn't have seen all the parallels between this story and Watterson's larger feelings about the strip. His notice to readers, announcing the strip's end, wouldn't be published for another month. But this piece, which is quintessential *Calvin and Hobbes*, illustrated yet again a common experience that is felt exponentially harder during childhood. The passage of time is gradual, and relentless, and comes for us all. It's possible to read Calvin's side of the argument as a caricature of fan entitlement — his final line, "I like to have everything so good, I can take it all for granted," seems to invite it. Yet this has been Calvin since the strip's debut: a fire hose of imagination who can't sit still or wait for anything or anyone. And he's always exactly, precisely counterbalanced on the page by Hobbes, the sage big-picture thinker who has no inborn loyalty to humans, but who enjoys hanging out with them anyway. Like so many other strips, this particular argument had a topical resonance, but it was really about so much more. No, the good things don't last forever. But at least they happened.

So how will the strip be remembered? It's already had so much ink spilled in its name — anointing it as everything from "an indelible and truly child-centric view of the world"[108] to "our only popular explication of the moral philosophy of Aristotle"[109] — and it's likely there are even hotter takes that we can't yet fathom hiding just around the corner. How about this, for a start: *Calvin and Hobbes* is, if not North America's last great comic strip, then the last one with the power to unite readers around the world, across cultural and generational lines, and to serve as the kind of artistic and intellectual totem that millions of parents will reverentially pass on to their own children when the time is right. That's partly because the medium that birthed it is currently in the throes of a painful self-destruction. But it's also a testament to Watterson having been in the right place, at the right time, with the right skills — and, most of all, the right idea.

And even if the strip *does* disappear from public consciousness, with all tens of millions of books suddenly turned to ash and every *Calvin and Hobbes* fan struck with an extremely specific type of amnesia — well, maybe even *that* isn't so bad. In 1990, Watterson made what turned out to be his final public appearance when he delivered the commencement speech at his alma mater, Kenyon College. Rather than do any dishing about *Calvin and Hobbes*, though — he didn't so much as name the title of his strip — Watterson talked at length about the dangers of corporate greed and the importance of having ethics in a world that doesn't put any kind of premium on them. (A familiar song, to anyone who'd seen the show before.) But he also told a story about the time he painted a copy of Michelangelo's *The Creation of Adam* on the ceiling of his dorm room in his sophomore year. It was an arduous process, he told the crowd, involving a homemade scaffolding system made of chairs and a table stolen from the hall lounge, and it took Watterson nearly the entire school year to complete. Nobody would have mistaken it for a work of beauty, either. "But what the work lacked in color sense and technical flourish," Watterson said, "it gained in the incongruity of having a High Renaissance masterpiece in a college dorm that had the unmistakeable odor of old beer cans and older laundry."[110]

At some point, Watterson realized he should probably get permission for this little project of his. He asked the housing director, fudged his proposed start date by a couple of months, and was eventually told that the painting was allowed — so long as he painted over it and restored the ceiling to its usual state by the end of the school year, by then only a few weeks away. But for Watterson, the fact that his painting was doomed to be covered up and forgotten didn't diminish its importance. It also didn't diminish how much fun he had making it. "Despite the futility of the whole episode," Watterson said, "my fondest memories of college are times like these, where things were done out of some inexplicable inner imperative, rather than because the work was demanded . . . It's surprising how hard we'll work when the work is done just for ourselves."[111]

Obviously, *Calvin and Hobbes* required a lot more rigor and adherence to rules than a Michelangelo impersonation on a smelly-dorm-room ceiling. But there's something familiar about Watterson's quest to bring high art and sophisticated goofiness into a place where you wouldn't expect to find it. The spirit that animated him during his college years is exactly what would later motivate his six-year-old hero. You create for creation's sake. And if you happen to find someone who can see what you see — well, you've hit the jackpot, haven't you?

"The mind is like a car battery," Watterson told his audience at Kenyon. "It recharges by running." He's right. Our imaginations don't disintegrate in adulthood; they only atrophy with neglect. There are always ways of restrengthening those muscles. Reading *Calvin and Hobbes* is one of them. That kind of regeneration-via-imagination is what led Calvin to invent a sport where almost literally anything can happen, and it's what sent him crash-landing on distant moons in the middle of math class. Imagination is also what got Calvin to take off on his sled, time after time, pondering the nature of free will with a six-foot-tall tiger in tow.

He's not coming back, but we know he'll find something special wherever he winds up. He always does.

*Endnotes

1 *Dear Mr. Watterson*, directed by Joel Allen Schroeder (2013), iTunes.

2 Bill Watterson, *The Calvin and Hobbes Tenth Anniversary Book* (Kansas City: Andrews and McMeel, 1995), 22.

3 Andrew Christie, "An Interview with Bill Watterson," *Honk*, 1987.

4 Watterson, *The Calvin and Hobbes Tenth Anniversary Book*, 22.

5 Bill Watterson, *Exploring Calvin and Hobbes: An Exhibition Catalogue* (Kansas City: Andrews McMeel, 2014), 1.

6 Watterson, *Exploring Calvin and Hobbes*, 3.

7 Bill Watterson, *The Complete Calvin and Hobbes*, vol. 1 (Kansas City: Andrews McMeel, 2012), 6.

8 Watterson, *The Complete Calvin and Hobbes*, vol. 1, 6.

9 Watterson, *Exploring Calvin and Hobbes*, 6.

10 Watterson, *The Complete Calvin and Hobbes*, vol. 1, 7.

11 Watterson, *Exploring Calvin and Hobbes*, 9.

12 Watterson, *Exploring Calvin and Hobbes*, 9.

13 Watterson, *Exploring Calvin and Hobbes*, 10.

14 Nevin Martell, *Looking for Calvin and Hobbes* (New York: Bloomsbury, 2009), 62.

15 Richard Samuel West, "Interview: Bill Watterson," *The Comics Journal*, February 1989.

16 Watterson, *The Calvin and Hobbes Tenth Anniversary Book*, 68.

17 Watterson, *The Calvin and Hobbes Tenth Anniversary Book*, 84.

18 Jorge Luis Borges, "The Analytical Language of John Wilkins," in *Other Inquisitions (1937–1952)*, trans. Ruth L. C. Simms (Austin: University of Texas Press, 1964), 103.

19 Watterson, *The Calvin and Hobbes Tenth Anniversary Book*, 54.

20 Watterson, *The Calvin and Hobbes Tenth Anniversary Book*, 129.

21 Bill Watterson, *Calvin and Hobbes* (Kansas City: Andrews and McMeel, 1987), 3–4.

22 Christie, "An Interview with Bill Watterson."

23 Christie, "An Interview with Bill Watterson."

24 Christie, "An Interview with Bill Watterson."

25 Martell, *Looking for Calvin and Hobbes*, 64.

26 West, "Interview: Bill Watterson."

27 West, "Interview: Bill Watterson."

28 West, "Interview: Bill Watterson."

29 West, "Interview: Bill Watterson."

30 Martell, *Looking for Calvin and Hobbes*, 89.

31 Watterson, *The Complete Calvin and Hobbes*, vol. 1, 13.

32 Watterson, *The Complete Calvin and Hobbes*, vol. 1, 14.

33 Lee Salem, interview with the author, February 15, 2017.

34 Watterson, *The Complete Calvin and Hobbes*, vol. 1, 14.

35 Watterson, *The Complete Calvin and Hobbes*, vol. 1, 14.

36 Martell, *Looking for Calvin and Hobbes*, 146.

37 Watterson, *Exploring Calvin and Hobbes*, 12.

38 Martell, *Looking for Calvin and Hobbes*, 143.

39 Watterson, *The Calvin and Hobbes Tenth Anniversary Book*, 147.

40 Watterson, *The Calvin and Hobbes Tenth Anniversary Book*, 148.

41 Neal Rubin, "Comic Strip Coming Back, Bigger than Anyone Else's," *Hamilton Spectator*, January 30, 1992.

42 Watterson, *Exploring Calvin and Hobbes*, 15.

43 Watterson, *The Calvin and Hobbes Tenth Anniversary Book*, 166.

44 Watterson, *The Calvin and Hobbes Tenth Anniversary Book*, 76.

45 Watterson, *The Calvin and Hobbes Tenth Anniversary Book*, 27.

46 Rubin, "Comic Strip Coming Back, Bigger than Anyone Else's."

47 Salem, interview with the author, February 15, 2017.

48 Watterson, *Exploring Calvin and Hobbes*, 26.

49 Martell, *Looking for Calvin and Hobbes*, 152–53.

50 Watterson, *The Calvin and Hobbes Tenth Anniversary Book*, 104.

51 Andrews McMeel Publishing, "Contact Us," publishing.andrewsmcmeel.com/our-company/contact-us.

52 Alison Flood, "George RR Martin Gives Impatient Readers the Finger," *The Guardian*, July 10, 2014, www.theguardian.com/books/2014/jul/10/george-rr-martin-tells-readers-fuck-off-game-of-thrones.

53 John Campanelli, "'Calvin and Hobbes' Fans Still Pine 15 Years After Its Exit," *Cleveland Plain Dealer*, February 1, 2010.

54 Watterson, *The Complete Calvin and Hobbes*, vol. 1, 16.

55 Lane Hartill, "Cartoonist Bill Watterson," *Christian Science Monitor*, December 28, 2000.

56 Martell, *Looking for Calvin and Hobbes*, 7.

57 Martell, *Looking for Calvin and Hobbes*, 218.

58 Martell, *Looking for Calvin and Hobbes*, 220.

59 Nicolas Rapold, "The Genius Behind the Subversive Squiggles," *New York Times*, November 14, 2013.

60 Bill Watterson, "Drawn into a Dark but Gentle World," *Los Angeles Times*, December 21, 1999.

61 Bill Watterson, "The Grief that Made 'Peanuts' Good," *Wall Street Journal*, October 12, 2007.

62 Bill Watterson, *Calvin and Hobbes: Sunday Pages 1985–1995* (Kansas City: Andrews McMeel, 2001), 7.

63 Watterson, *Calvin and Hobbes: Sunday Pages*, 7.

64 John Hodgman, "Comics Chronicle," *New York Times*, December 4, 2005.

65 Watterson, *The Complete Calvin and Hobbes*, vol. 1, 5.

66 Watterson, *The Complete Calvin and Hobbes*, vol. 1, 16.

67 Watterson, *The Complete Calvin and Hobbes*, vol. 1, 17.

68 Watterson, *The Complete Calvin and Hobbes*, vol. 1, 17.

69 Watterson, *The Complete Calvin and Hobbes*, vol. 1, 18.

70 John Campanelli, "Bill Watterson, Creator of Beloved 'Calvin and Hobbes' Comic Strip, Looks Back with No Regrets," *Cleveland Plain Dealer*, February 1, 2010.

71 Michael Cavna, "THIS JUST IN: First New Art from 'Calvin and Hobbes' Creator in 16 Years, Syndicate Says," *Washington Post*, April 22, 2011.

72 *Stripped*, directed by Dave Kellett and Frederick Schroeder (2014), iTunes.

73 Stephan Pastis, "Ever Wished That Calvin and Hobbes Creator Bill Watterson Would Return to the Comics Page? Well, He Just Did," *Pearls Before Swine: The Blog O' Stephan Pastis*, June 7, 2014.

74 Salem, interview with the author, February 15, 2017.

75 Michael Cavna, "Bill Watterson Talks: This Is Why You Must Read the New 'Exploring Calvin and Hobbes' Book," *Washington Post*, March 9, 2015.

76 Watterson, *Exploring Calvin and Hobbes*, 5.

77 Watterson, *Exploring Calvin and Hobbes*, 31.

78 Watterson, *Exploring Calvin and Hobbes*, 35.

79 Salem, interview with the author, February 15, 2017.

80 *Stripped*, directed by Dave Kellett and Frederick Schroeder.

81 *Stripped*, directed by Dave Kellett and Frederick Schroeder.

82 Watterson, "Drawn into a Dark but Gentle World."

83 Salem, interview with the author, February 15, 2017.

84 Christie, "An Interview with Bill Watterson."

85 Adam Bernstein, "Race Fans Crazy for 'Calvin,'" *Chicago Tribune*, August 21, 1997.

86 Phil Edwards, "The Tasteless History of the Peeing Calvin Decal," *Trivia Happy*, July 2, 2014.

87 Hank Stuever, "The Whiz Kid: An Examination of the Truck Wars, the Redneck Mind-set and the Taking of a Beloved Comic-strip Character," *Austin American Statesman*, May 28, 1999.

88 Dave Philipps, "Whiz Kid: Cartoon Image Co-opted as a Symbol for All Sorts of Social Commentary," *Gazette* (Colorado Springs, Co.), March 21, 2004.

89 Stuever, "The Whiz Kid."

90 Stuever, "The Whiz Kid."

91 "'Peeing Calvin' Decals Now Recognized as Vital Channel of National Discourse," *The Onion*, April 5, 2000.

92 Jake Rossen, "Our Interview with *Calvin and Hobbes* Creator Bill Watterson!" *Mental Floss*, December 2013.

93 Frank Ahrens, "So Long, Kid: An Obituary for a Boy, His Tiger and Our Innocence," *Washington Post*, November 19, 1995.

94 Joey Morona, "Calvin and Hobbes Return as Residents of 'Bloom County,'" *Cleveland Plain Dealer*, April 1, 2016.

95 Michael Cavna, "'Lio' Creator Mark Tatulli Shares the Secrets of Spoofing 'Calvin and Hobbes,'" *Washington Post*, August 11, 2010.

96 Martell, *Looking for Calvin and Hobbes*, 175.

97 *Dear Mr. Watterson*, directed by Joel Allen Schroeder.

98 *Dear Mr. Watterson*, directed by Joel Allen Schroeder.

99 Stubby the Rocket, "*Hobbes & Me* Is Like Getting a Hug from a Tiger, in a Good Way," *Tor*, April 26, 2016.

100 Martine Leavitt, *Calvin* (Toronto: Groundwood, 2015), 19.

101 Leavitt, *Calvin*, 15.

102 Leavitt, *Calvin*, 31.

103 Leavitt, *Calvin*, 48.

104 Leavitt, *Calvin*, 101.

105 Leavitt, *Calvin*, 68.

106 Leavitt, *Calvin*, 79.

107 Leavitt, *Calvin*, 114.

108 Michael Agger, "What We're Reading," *New Yorker*, November 12, 2012.

109 James Q. Wilson, "'Calvin and Hobbes' and the Moral Sense," *Weekly Standard*, December 17, 1995.

110 Bill Watterson, Kenyon College commencement speech, 1990.

111 Watterson, Kenyon College commencement speech.

Acknowledgments

Thanks to Jen Knoch, Crissy Calhoun, and everyone else at ECW for letting me be part of the Pop Classics family. Avril McMeekin remembered the en dashes every time I forgot them. Vivek Shraya shared notes and encouragement. Monsieur Sabourin's grade-four class in southwest Edmonton voted on the cover color. Mike Yingling's full-text *Calvin and Hobbes* search engine was a constant godsend. And Bridget and Finn have now inherited all my old books — if anyone tries the *pair o' pathetic peripatetics* line, I know you'll be ready.

Michael Hingston's writing has appeared in *Wired* magazine, the *Washington Post*, and the *Guardian*. His novel *The Dilettantes* was a #1 regional bestseller. He is also co-creator of the Short Story Advent Calendar. Hingston lives in Edmonton.